The Poetry of Thomas Parnell

Volume I

The Poet Thomas Parnell was born in Ireland on 11th September 1679. He was the descendant of an ancient family, which had been settled for hundreds of years at Congleton in Cheshire. His father, also named Thomas, took the side of the Commonwealth, and at the Restoration went over to Ireland, where he purchased a considerable property. This, along with his estate in Cheshire, devolved to the poet and was to provide an income of rents with which the young Parnell could embrace life.

At school he is said to have distinguished himself by the retentiveness of his memory; often performing the task allotted for days in a few hours, and being able to repeat forty lines in any book of poems, after the first reading.

He entered Trinity College Dublin at the unusually early age of thirteen and took the degree of M.A. in 1700. The same year (although a dispensation was needed on account of his being under age) he was ordained deacon by the Bishop of Derry. Three years after, he was ordained a priest; and in 1705, he was made Archdeacon of Clogher, by Sir George Ashe, bishop of that see.

On receipt of the archdeanery, he married Miss Ann Minchin, described as a young lady of great beauty, and of an amiable character, by whom he had two sons, who tragically, died young, and a daughter, who was to survive both parents.

Up to the fall of the Whigs, at the end of Queen Anne's reign, Parnell appears to have been, like his father, a keen supporter. He now switched political allegiance to the Tories and was hailed as a valuable addition to their ranks.

Parnell was blessed with great social qualities and soon fell in with the brilliant set of literary figures; Pope, Swift, Gay. He became a member of the Scriblerus Club , an informal gathering of authors, based in London, in the early 18th century. Prominent figures from the Augustan Age of English letters were members; Jonathan Swift, Alexander Pope, John Gay, John Arbuthnot and Henry St. John. Founded in 1714 the club lasted until the death of the founders, finally ending in 1745. At about his time Parnell also wrote in the "Spectator."

To Pope, he was of essential service, assisting him in his notes to the "Iliad," being, what Pope was not, a good Greek scholar. He wrote a life of Homer, which was prefixed to the Translation, although stiff in style, and flamboyant in statement.

Parnell first visited London in 1706; and from that period till his death, scarcely a year elapsed without his spending some time in the great metropolis.

As soon as he had collected his rents, he would travel to London to enjoy himself though he continued to preach and his sermons were popular even if it appears they were more of the 'showman' type.

As each London furlough expired, he returned to Ireland, jaded and dispirited, and there took delight in nursing his melancholy; in pining for the amusements of what he had left behind; shunning and sneering at the society around him; and in abusing his native bogs and his fellow-countrymen in verse.

In 1712 he lost his wife, with whom he appears to have lived as happily as his morbid temperament and mortified feelings would permit. This blow deepened his melancholy, and drove him, it is said, to excessive drinking.

Later that same year and back in London, and once more under the "special patronage" of Dean Swift, and who wished, through his side, to mortify certain persons in Ireland, who did not appreciate, he says, the Archdeacon; and who, we suspect, besides, did not thoroughly appreciate the Dean. Swift, partly in pity for the "poor lad," as he calls him, whom he saw to be in such imminent danger of losing caste and character, and partly in the true patronising spirit, introduced Parnell to Lord Bolingbroke, who received him kindly, entertained him at dinner, and encouraged him in his poetical studies but did little else. The consequences of dissipation began, at this time, too, to appear in Parnell's constitution; and we find Swift saying of him, "His head is out of order, like mine, but more constant, poor boy." It was perhaps to this period that Pope referred, when he told Spence, "Parnell is a great follower of drams, and strangely open and scandalous in his debaucheries." If so, his bad habits seem to have sprung as much from disappointment and discontent as from taste.

Yet Swift continued to help his friend, and it was at his instance that, in 1713, Archbishop King presented Parnell with a prebend (a portion of the revenues of a cathedral or collegiate church formerly granted to a canon or member of the chapter as his stipend).

In 1714, his hope of London promotion died with Queen Anne; but in 1716, the same generous Archbishop bestowed on him the vicarage of Finglass, in the diocese of Dublin, worth £400 a-year.

However Thomas Parnell did not live long enough to enjoy the full benefit. He died at Chester, about to leave for Ireland, on 24 October 1718.

As a poet his legacy was not of the first order but his poems were greatly appreciated as were his skills as essayist and translator and obviously as a clergyman his talents seemed to have ensured promotion but quite how observant he was given his excess is difficult to judge.

Parnell's poetry is lyrical and often is written in heroic couplets. It was said of his poetry 'it was in keeping with his character, easy and pleasing, enunciating the common places with felicity and grace.' He was also one of the so-called "Graveyard poets": his 'A Night-Piece on Death,' widely considered the first "Graveyard School" poem, which was published posthumously in Poems on Several Occasions, collected and edited by his great friend Alexander Pope.

Index of Poems

A Night Piece on Death

By the blue taper's trembling light,
No more I waste the wakeful night,
Intent with endless view to pore
The schoolmen and the sages o'er:
Their books from wisdom widely stray,
Or point at best the longest way.
I'll seek a readier path, and go
Where wisdom's surely taught below.

How deep yon azure dyes the sky!
Where orbs of gold unnumber'd lie,
While through their ranks in silver pride
The nether crescent seems to glide!

The slumb'ring breeze forgets to breathe,
The lake is smooth and clear beneath,
Where once again the spangled show
Descends to meet our eyes below.
The grounds which on the right aspire,
In dimness from the view retire:
The left presents a place of graves,
Whose wall the silent water laves.
That steeple guides thy doubtful sight
Among the livid gleams of night.
There pass with melancholy state,
By all the solemn heaps of fate,
And think, as softly-sad you tread
Above the venerable dead,
"Time was, like thee they life possest,
And time shall be, that thou shalt rest."

Those graves, with bending osier bound,
That nameless heave the crumpled ground,
Quick to the glancing thought disclose,
Where toil and poverty repose.

The flat smooth stones that bear a name,
The chisel's slender help to fame,
(Which ere our set of friends decay
Their frequent steps may wear away,)
A middle race of mortals own,
Men, half ambitious, all unknown.

The marble tombs that rise on high,
Whose dead in vaulted arches lie,
Whose pillars swell with sculptur'd stones,
Arms, angels, epitaphs, and bones,
These (all the poor remains of state)
Adorn the rich, or praise the great;
Who, while on earth in fame they live,
Are senseless of the fame they give.

Ha! while I gaze, pale Cynthia fades,
The bursting earth unveils the shades!
All slow, and wan, and wrapp'd with shrouds
They rise in visionary crowds,
And all with sober accent cry,
"Think, mortal, what it is to die."

Now from yon black and fun'ral yew,
That bathes the charnel-house with dew,
Methinks I hear a voice begin;
(Ye ravens, cease your croaking din;
Ye tolling clocks, no time resound
O'er the long lake and midnight ground)

It sends a peal of hollow groans,
Thus speaking from among the bones.

"When men my scythe and darts supply,
How great a king of fears am I!
They view me like the last of things:
They make, and then they dread, my stings.
Fools! if you less provok'd your fears,
No more my spectre form appears.
Death's but a path that must be trod,
If man would ever pass to God;
A port of calms, a state of ease
From the rough rage of swelling seas.

"Why then thy flowing sable stoles,
Deep pendant cypress, mourning poles,
Loose scarfs to fall athwart thy weeds,
Long palls, drawn hearses, cover'd steeds,
And plumes of black, that, as they tread,
Nod o'er the scutcheons of the dead?

"Nor can the parted body know,
Nor wants the soul, these forms of woe.
As men who long in prison dwell,
With lamps that glimmer round the cell,
Whene'er their suff'ring years are run,
Spring forth to greet the glitt'ring sun:
Such joy though far transcending sense,
Have pious souls at parting hence.
On earth, and in the body plac'd,
A few, and evil years they waste;
But when their chains are cast aside,
See the glad scene unfolding wide,
Clap the glad wing, and tow'r away,
And mingle with the blaze of day."

The Judgement of Paris

Where waving Pines the brows of Ida shade,
The swain young Paris half supinely laid,
Saw the loose Flocks thro' shrubs unnumber'd rove
And Piping call'd them to the gladded grove.
'Twas there he met the Message of the skies,
That he the Judge of Beauty deal the prize.

The Message known, one Love with anxious mind,
To make his Mother guard the time assign'd,
Drew forth her proud white Swans, and trac'd the pair
That wheel her Chariot in the purple air:

A golden Bow behind his shoulder bends,
A golden Quiver at his side depends,
Pointing to these he nods, with fearless State,
And bids her safely meet the grand Debate.
Another Love proceeds with anxious care
To make his Iv'ry sleek the shining hair,
Moves the loose Curls and bids the Forehead shew
In full Expansion all its native snow.
A third enclasps the many colour'd Cest
And rul'd by Fancy sets the silver Vest,
When to her Sons with intermingl'd sighs
The Goddess of the rosy lips applies.

'Tis now my darling boys a time to shew
The love you feel, the filial aids you owe:
Yet would we think that any dar'd to strive
For Charms, when Venus and her Loves alive?
Or should the prize of beauty be deni'd,
Has Beauty's Empress ought to boast beside?
And ting'd with Poison, pleasing while it harms,
My Darts I trusted to your infant arms;
If, when your hands have arch'd the golden Bow,
The World's great Ruler bending owns the blow,
Let no contending Form invade my due,
Tall Juno's Mein, nor Pallas Eyes of blew.
But grac'd with Triumph, to the Paphian shore,
Your Venus bears the Palms of Conquest o'er,
And joyful see my hundred Altars there
With costly Gums perfume the wanton air.

While thus the Cupids hear the Cyprian Dame,
The groves resounded where a Goddess came.
The warlike Pallas march'd with mighty stride,
Her Shield forgot, her Helmet laid aside.
Her Hair unbound, in curls and order flow'd,
And Peace, or something like, her Visage shew'd;
So with her eyes serene and hopeful haste,
The long stretch'd Allys of the Wood she trac'd.
But where the Woods a second Entrance found,
With Scepter'd Pomp, and Golden Glory crown'd
The stately Juno stalk'd, to reach the Seat,
And hear the Sentence in the last Debate,
And long, severely long resent the Grove;
In this, what boots it, she's the wife of Jove.

Arm'd with a Grace, at length, secure to win,
The lovely Venus smiling enters in;
All sweet and shining near the Youth she drew,
Her rosy Neck ambrosial odours threw;
The sacred Scents diffus'd among the leaves,
Ran down the Woods and fill'd their hoary Caves;

The Charms, so am'rous all, and each so great,
The conquer'd Judge no longer keeps his Seat;
Oppress'd with Light, he drops his weary'd eyes
And fears he should be thought to doubt the Prize.

An Elegy, To an Old Beauty

In vain, poor Nymph, to please our youthful sight
You sleep in cream and frontlets all the night,
Your face with patches soil, with paint repair,
Dress with gay gowns, and shade with foreign hair.
If truth in spight of manners must be told,
Why, really fifty-five is something old.

Once you were young; or one, whose life's so long
She might have born my mother, tells me wrong.
And once (since Envy's dead before you die,)
The women own, you play'd a sparkling eye,
Taught the light foot a modish little trip,
And pouted with the prettiest purple lip

To some new charmer are the roses fled,
Which blew, to damask all thy cheek with red;
Youth calls the Graces there to fix their reign,
And airs by thousands fill their easy train.
So parting Summer bids her flow'ry prime
Attend the sun to dress some foreign clime,
While with'ring seasons in succession, here,
Strip the gay gardens, and deform the year.

But thou (since Nature bids) the world resign,
'Tis now thy daughter's daughter's time to shine.
With more address, (or such as pleases more)
She runs her female exercises o'er,
Unfurls or closes, raps or turns the Fan,
And smiles, or blushes at the creature Man.
With quicker life, as guilded coaches pass,
In sideling courtesy she drops the glass.

With better strength, on visit-days she bears
To mount her fifty flights of ample stairs.
Her mein, her shape, her temper, eyes and tongue
Are sure to conquer for the rogue is young;
And all that's madly wild, or oddly gay,
We call it only pretty Fanny's way.

Let time that makes you homely, make you sage,
The sphere of wisdom is the sphere of age.
'Tis true, when beauty dawns with early fire,

And hears the flatt'ring tongues of soft desire,
If not from virtue, from its gravest ways
The soul with pleasing avocation strays.
But beauty gone, 'tis easier to be wise;
As harper better, by the loss of eyes.

Henceforth retire, reduce your roving airs,
Haunt less the plays, and more the publick pray'rs,
Reject the Mechlin Head, and gold brocade,
Go pray, in sober Norwich Crape array'd.
Thy pendent diamonds let thy Fanny take,
(Their trembling lustre shows how much you shake;)
Or bid her wear thy necklace row'd with pearl,
You'll find your Fanny an obedient girl.

So for the rest, with less incumbrance hung,
You walk thro' life, unmingled with the young;
And view the shade and substance as you pass
With joint endeavour trifling at the glass,
Or Folly drest, and rambling all her days,
To meet her counterpart, and grow by praise:
Yet still sedate your self, and gravely plain,
You neither fret, nor envy at the vain.

'Twas thus (if Man with Woman we compare)
The wise Athenian crost a glittering fair,
Unmov'd by tongues and sights, he walk'd the place,
Thro' tape, toys, tinsel, gimp, perfume, and lace;
Then bends from Mars's Hill his awful eyes,
And "What a world I never want?" he cries;
But cries unheard: For Folly will be free.
So parts the buzzing gaudy crowd, and he:
As careless he for them, as they for him;
He wrapt in wisdom, and they whirl'd by whim.

A Hymn to Contentment

Lovely, lasting peace of mind!
Sweet delight of human-kind!
Heavenly-born, and bred on high,
To crown the fav'rites of the sky
With more of happiness below,
Than victors in a triumph know!
Whither, O whither art thou fled,
To lay thy meek, contented head;
What happy region dost thou please
To make the seat of calms and ease!

Ambition searches all its sphere

Of pomp and state, to meet thee there.
Increasing Avarice would find
Thy presence in its gold enshrin'd.
The bold advent'rer ploughs his way
Through rocks amidst the foaming sea,
To gain thy love; and then perceives
Thou wert not in the rocks and waves.
The silent heart which grief assails,
Treads soft and lonesome o'er the vales,
Sees daisies open, rivers run,
And seeks (as I have vainly done)
Amusing thought; but learns to know
That solitude's the nurse of woe.
No real happiness is found
In trailing purple o'er the ground;
Or in a soul exalted high,
To range the circuit of the sky,
Converse with stars above, and know
All nature in its forms below;
The rest it seeks, in seeking dies,
And doubts at last, for knowledge, rise.

Lovely, lasting peace, appear!
This world itself, if thou art here,
Is once again with Eden blest,
And man contains it in his breast.

'Twas thus, as under shade I stood,
I sung my wishes to the wood,
And lost in thought, no more perceiv'd
The branches whisper as they wav'd:
It seem'd, as all the quiet place
Confess'd the presence of the Grace.
When thus she spoke "Go rule thy will,
Bid thy wild passions all be still,
Know God and bring thy heart to know
The joys which from religion flow:
Then ev'ry Grace shall prove its guest,
And I'll be there to crown the rest."

Oh! by yonder mossy seat,
In my hours of sweet retreat,
Might I thus my soul employ,
With sense of gratitude and joy!
Rais'd as ancient prophets were,
In heavenly vision, praise, and pray'r;
Pleasing all men, hurting none,
Pleas'd and bless'd with God alone:
Then while the gardens take my sight,
With all the colours of delight;
While silver waters glide along,

To please my ear, and court my song;
I'll lift my voice, and tune my string,
And thee, great source of nature, sing.

The sun that walks his airy way,
To light the world, and give the day;
The moon that shines with borrow'd light;
The stars that gild the gloomy night;
The seas that roll unnumber'd waves;
The wood that spreads its shady leaves;
The field whose ears conceal the grain,
The yellow treasure of the plain;
All of these, and all I see,
Should be sung, and sung by me:
They speak their maker as they can,
But want and ask the tongue of man.

Go search among your idle dreams,
Your busy or your vain extremes;
And find a life of equal bliss,
Or own the next begun in this.

The Hermit

Far in a wild, unknown to public view,
From youth to age a rev'rend hermit grew;
The moss his bed, the cave his humble cell,
His food the fruits, his drink the crystal well:
Remote from man, with God he pass'd the days,
Pray'r all his bus'ness, all his pleasure praise.

A life so sacred, such serene repose,
Seem'd heav'n itself, till one suggestion rose;
That vice should triumph, virtue vice obey,
This sprung some doubt of Providence's sway:
His hopes no more a certain prospect boast,
And all the tenor of his soul is lost.
So when a smooth expanse receives imprest
Calm nature's image on its wat'ry breast,
Down bend the banks, the trees depending grow,
And skies beneath with answering colours glow:
But if a stone the gentle scene divide,
Swift ruffling circles curl on ev'ry side,
And glimm'ring fragments of a broken sun,
Banks, trees, and skies, in thick disorder run.

To clear this doubt, to know the world by sight,
To find if books, or swains, report it right,
(For yet by swains alone the world he knew,

Whose feet came wand'ring o'er the nightly dew,)
He quits his cell; the pilgrim-staff he bore,
And fix'd the scallop in his hat before;
Then with the sun a rising journey went,
Sedate to think, and watching each event.

The morn was wasted in the pathless grass,
And long and lonesome was the wild to pass;
But when the southern sun had warm'd the day,
A youth came posting o'er a crossing way;
His raiment decent, his complexion fair,
And soft in graceful ringlets wav'd his hair.
Then near approaching, "Father, hail!" he cried;
"And hail, my son," the rev'rend sire replied;
Words follow'd words, from question answer flow'd,
And talk of various kind deceiv'd the road;
Till each with other pleas'd, and loth to part,
While in their age they differ, join in heart
Thus stands an aged elm in ivy bound,
Thus youthful ivy clasps an elm around.

Now sunk the sun; the closing hour of day
Came onward, mantled o'er with sober gray;
Nature in silence bid the world repose;
When near the road a stately palace rose:
There by the moon through ranks of trees they pass,
Whose verdure crown'd their sloping sides of grass.
It chanc'd the noble master of the dome
Still made his house the wand'ring stranger's home;
Yet still the kindness, from a thirst of praise,
Prov'd the vain flourish of expensive ease.
The pair arrive: the liv'ried servants wait;
Their lord receives them at the pompous gate.
The table groans with costly piles of food,
And all is more than hospitably good.
Then led to rest, the day's long toil they drown,
Deep sunk in sleep, and silk, and heaps of down.

At length 'tis morn, and at the dawn of day,
Along the wide canals the zephyrs play;
Fresh o'er the gay parterres the breezes creep,
And shake the neighb'ring wood to banish sleep.
Up rise the guests, obedient to the call:
An early banquet deck'd the splendid hall;
Rich luscious wine a golden goblet grac'd,
Which the kind master forc'd the guests to taste.
Then, pleas'd and thankful, from the porch they go;
And, but the landlord, none had cause of woe;
His cup was vanish'd; for in secret guise
The younger guest purloin'd the glitt'ring prize.

As one who spies a serpent in his way,
Glist'ning and basking in the summer ray,
Disorder'd stops to shun the danger near,
Then walks with faintness on, and looks with fear;
So seem'd the sire; when far upon the road,
The shining spoil his wily partner show'd.
He stopp'd with silence, walk'd with trembling heart,
And much he wish'd, but durst not ask to part:
Murmuring he lifts his eyes, and thinks it hard,
That gen'rous actions meet a base reward.

While thus they pass, the sun his glory shrouds,
The changing skies hang out their sable clouds;
A sound in air presag'd approaching rain,
And beasts to covert scud across the plain.
Warn'd by the signs, the wand'ring pair retreat,
To seek for shelter at a neighb'ring seat.
'Twas built with turrets, on a rising ground,
And strong, and large, and unimprov'd around;
Its owner's temper, tim'rous and severe,
Unkind and griping, caus'd a desert there.

As near the miser's heavy doors they drew,
Fierce rising gusts with sudden fury blew;
The nimble lightning mix'd with showers began,
And o'er their heads loud rolling thunders ran.
Here long they knock, but knock or call in vain,
Driven by the wind, and batter'd by the rain.
At length some pity warm'd the master's breast,
('Twas then his threshold first receiv'd a guest,)
Slow creaking turns the door with jealous care,
And half he welcomes in the shiv'ring pair;
One frugal faggot lights the naked walls,
And Nature's fervour through their limbs recalls:
Bread of the coarsest sort, with eager wine,
Each hardly granted, serv'd them both to dine;
And when the tempest first appear'd to cease,
A ready warning bid them part in peace.
With still remark the pond'ring hermit view'd
In one so rich, a life so poor and rude;
And why should such, within himself he cried,
Lock the lost wealth a thousand want beside?
But what new marks of wonder soon took place
In every settling feature of his face,
When from his vest the young companion bore
That cup, the gen'rous landlord own'd before,
And paid profusely with the precious bowl,
The stinted kindness of this churlish soul!

But now the clouds in airy tumult fly;
The sun emerging opes an azure sky;

A fresher green the smelling leaves display,
And glitt'ring as they tremble, cheer the day:
The weather courts them from their poor retreat,
And the glad master bolts the wary gate.

While hence they walk, the pilgrim's bosom wrought:
WIth all the travel of uncertain thought;
His partner's acts without their cause appear,
'Twas there a vice, and seem'd a madness here:
Detesting that, and pitying this, he goes,
Lost and confounded with the various shows.

Now night's dim shades again involve the sky,
Again the wanderers want a place to lie,
Again they search, and find a lodging nigh:
The soil improv'd around, the mansion neat,
And neither poorly low, nor idly great:
It seem'd to speak its master's turn of mind,
Content, and not for praise, but virtue kind.

Hither the walkers turn with weary feet,
Then bless the mansion, and the master greet:
Their greeting fair bestow'd, with modest guise,
The courteous master hears, and thus replies:

"Without a vain, without a grudging heart,
To Him who gives us all, I yield a part;
From Him you come, for Him accept it here,
A frank and sober, more than costly cheer."
He spoke, and bid the welcome table spread,
Then talk'd of virtue till the time of bed,
When the grave household round his hall repair,
Warn'd by a bell, and close the hours with pray'r.

At length the world, renew'd by calm repose,
Was strong for toil, the dappled morn arose.
Before the pilgrims part, the younger crept
Near the clos'd cradle where an infant slept,
And writh'd his neck: the landlord's little pride,
O strange return! grew black, and gasp'd, and died!
Horrors of horrors! what! his only son!
How look'd our hermit when the fact was done?
Not hell, though hell's black jaws in sunder part,
And breathe blue fire, could more assault his heart.

Confus'd, and struck with silence at the deed,
He flies, but, trembling, fails to fly with speed.
His steps the youth pursues: the country lay
Perplex'd with roads, a servant show'd the way:
A river cross'd the path; the passage o'er
Was nice to find; the servant trod before:

Long arms of oak an open bridge supplied,
And deep the waves beneath the bending glide.
The youth, who seem'd to watch a time to sin,
Approach'd the careless guide, and thrust him in;
Plunging he falls, and rising lifts his head,
Then flashing turns, and sinks among the dead.

Wild, sparkling rage inflames the father's eyes,
He bursts the bands of fear, and madly cries,
"Detested wretch!" but scarce his speech began,
When the strange partner seem'd no longer man:
His youthful face grew more serenely sweet;
His robe turn'd white, and flow'd upon his feet,
Fair rounds of radiant points invest his hair;
Celestial odours breathe through purpled air;
And wings, whose colours glitter'd on the day,
Wide at his back their gradual plumes display.
The form ethereal bursts upon his sight,
And moves in all the majesty of light.

Though loud at first the pilgrim's passion grew,
Sudden he gaz'd, and wist not what to do;
Surprise in secret chains his words suspends,
And in a calm his settling temper ends.
But silence here the beauteous angel broke,
(The voice of music ravish'd as he spoke).

"Thy prayer, thy praise, thy life to vice unknown,
In sweet memorial rise before the throne:
These charms, success in our bright region find,
And force an angel down, to calm thy mind;
For this, commission'd, I forsook the sky,
Nay, cease to kneel thy fellow-servant I.

"Then know the truth of government divine,
And let these scruples be no longer thine.

"The Maker justly claims that world He made,
In this the right of Providence is laid;
Its sacred majesty through all depends
On using second means to work his ends:
'Tis thus, withdrawn in state from human eye,
The Pow'r exerts his attributes on high,
Your actions uses, nor controls your will,
And bids the doubting sons of men be still.

"What strange events can strike with more surprise,
Than those which lately struck thy wond'ring eyes?
Yet taught by these, confess th' Almighty just,
And where you can't unriddle, learn to trust!

"The great vain man, who far'd on costly food,
Whose life was too luxurious to be good;
Who made his iv'ry stands with goblets shine,
And forc'd his guests to morning draughts of wine,
Has, with the cup, the graceless custom lost,
And still he welcomes, but with less of cost.

"The mean, suspicious wretch, whose bolted door
Ne'er mov'd in duty to the wand'ring poor;
With him I left the cup, to teach his mind
That Heav'n can bless, if mortals will be kind.
Conscious of wanting worth, he views the bowl,
And feels compassion touch his grateful soul.
Thus artists melt the sullen ore of lead,
With heaping coals of fire upon its head;
In the kind warmth the metal learns to glow,
And loose from dross, the silver runs below.

"Long had our pious friend in virtue trod,
But now the child half-wean'd his heart from God;
(Child of his age) for him he liv'd in pain,
And measur'd back his steps to earth again.
To what excesses had this dotage run!
But God, to save the father, took the son.
To all but thee, in fits he seem'd to go,
(And 'twas my ministry to deal the blow).
The poor fond parent, humbled in the dust,
Now owns in tears the punishment was just.

"But how had all his fortune felt a wrack,
Had that false servant sped in safety back!
This night his treasur'd heaps he meant to steal,
And what a fund of charity would fail!

"Thus Heav'n instructs thy mind: this trial o'er,
Depart in peace, resign, and sin no more."

On sounding pinions here the youth withdrew,
The sage stood wondering as the seraph flew.
Thus look'd Elisha, when, to mount on high,
His master took the chariot of the sky;
The fiery pomp ascending left the view;
The prophet gaz'd, and wish'd to follow too.

The bending hermit here a prayer begun,
"Lord! as in heav'n, on earth thy will be done!"
Then gladly turning, sought his ancient place,
And pass'd a life of piety and peace.

A Beavy of the Fair & Gay

A Beavy of the fair & Gay,
Such as are daily Smoakt in tea,
& toasted over wine,
Vext to be made so long the Jeast
Of tongues & pens, to go in quest
Of reputation Joyn.
To K---d's house they first repair,
But scarce find any footsteps there,
to keep them off cold scent;
Long had she fled his slavery,
Her gallants stabbd him first, & she
Woud bury him in paint.
To O---y's they next advance,
But he was vanishd on a glance
to Make some conquest shott;
One who so many loves as she,
& one who loves fooles company,
Must love for you know what.
Of T---n newes in vain they sought,
Scarce M---ws covets to be thought
So ignorant in dressing;
For scandall had like Cr---fts appeard,
He urgd his suit, the God retird,
& left the Nymph unlacing.
No longer on your search remain,
For since your labour must be vain,
What need you make it long:
Believe me fairs, that every one
preserves him for her self alone,
Upon her proper tongue.

Psalm 51

Look mercyfully down O Lord
& wash us from our sinn
Cleanse us from wicked deeds without
from wicked thoughts within
Lord I Confess my many sinns
that I against thee doe
Each minute they're before my face
& wound my soul anew
So Great my god my ills have been
Gainst thee & onely thee
Thy Justice tho' I were Condemnd
would good & righteous bee
For att my birth I wickedness
Did with my breath suck in

But thou shalt teach me in thy ways
& keep me pure from sinn
Thoult me with hyssopp purge who am
all over soil's & stain's
Thou with thy sanctifiyng grace
shalt wash & make me clean
Thoult bless my days with peace no sound
But Joy shall reach mine ear
That where thy Justice wounded Lord
There Gladness may appear
Blott from thy thoughts past faults & from
The present turn thy face
O make my spirit right & good
Confirm my heart with grace
thy Presence & thy mercy lett
Me ever Ld possess
Me with the comfort of thy help
& with thy love still bless
Then shall the wicked know thy pow'r
& turn ym from theyr wayes
Deliver me from blood my god
& I will sing thy praise.
Unseal my lips & to ye Bad
I will thy mercy shew
For since thou lovest not sacrifice
Tis all that I can doo
A heart that is with sorrow pierct
My God thou wilt receive
this is ye sweetest offering
that we to thee can give
On Sion Graciously look down
Preserve us still we pray
& hearts upon thine altars Lord
Instead of beasts we'el Lay.

A Fairy Tale in the Ancient English Style

In Britain's Isle and Arthur's days,
When Midnight Faeries daunc'd the Maze,
Liv'd Edwin of the Green;
Edwin, I wis, a gentle Youth,
Endow'd with Courage, Sense and Truth,
Tho' badly Shap'd he been.
His Mountain Back mote well be said
To measure heigth against his Head,
And lift it self above:
Yet spite of all that Nature did
To make his uncouth Form forbid,
This Creature dar'd to love.

He felt the Charms of Edith's Eyes,
Nor wanted Hope to gain the Prize,
Cou'd Ladies took within;
But one Sir Topaz dress'd with Art,
And, if a Shape cou'd win a Heart,
He had a Shape to win.
Edwin (if right I read my Song)
With slighted Passion pac'd along
All in the Moony Light:
'Twas near an old enchaunted Court,
Where sportive Faeries made Resort
To revel out the Night.
His Heart was drear, his Hope was cross'd,
'Twas late, 'twas farr, the Path was lost
That reach'd the Neighbour-Town;
With weary Steps he quits the Shades,
Resolv'd the darkling Dome he treads,
And drops his Limbs adown.
But scant he lays him on the Floor,
When hollow Winds remove the Door,
A trembling rocks the Ground:
And (well I ween to count aright)
At once an hundred Tapers light
On all the Walls around.
Now sounding Tongues assail his Ear,
Now sounding Feet approachen near,
And now the Sounds encrease:
And from the Corner where he lay
He sees a Train profusely gay
Come pranckling o'er the Place.
But (trust me Gentles!) never yet
Was dight a Masquing half so neat,
Or half so rich before;
The Country lent the sweet Perfumes,
The Sea the Pearl, the Sky the Plumes,
The Town its silken Store.
Now whilst he gaz'd, a Gallant drest
In flaunting Robes above the rest,
With awfull Accent cry'd;
What Mortall of a wretched Mind,
Whose Sighs infect the balmy Wind,
Has here presum'd to hide?
At this the Swain whose vent'rous Soul
No Fears of Magick Art controul,
Advanc'd in open sight;
'Nor have I Cause of Dreed, he said,
'Who view by no Presumption led
'Your Revels of the Night.
''Twas Grief, for Scorn of faithful Love,
'Which made my Steps unweeting rove
'Amid the nightly Dew.

'Tis well, the Gallant crys again,
We Faeries never injure Men
Who dare to tell us true.
Exalt thy Love-dejected Heart,
Be mine the Task, or e'er we part,
To make thee Grief resign;
Now take the Pleasure of thy Chaunce;
Whilst I with Mab my part'ner daunce,
Be little Mable thine.

He spoke, and all a sudden there
Light Musick floats in wanton Air;
The Monarch leads the Queen:
The rest their Faerie Partners found,
And Mable trimly tript the Ground
With Edwin of the Green.

The Dauncing past, the Board was laid,
And siker such a Feast was made
As Heart and Lip desire;
Withouten Hands the Dishes fly,
The Glasses with a Wish come nigh,
And with a Wish retire.

But now to please the Faerie King,
Full ev'ry deal they laugh and sing,
And antick Feats devise;
Some wind and tumble like an Ape,
And other-some transmute their Shape
In Edwin's wond'ring Eyes.

'Till one at last that Robin hight,
(Renown'd for pinching Maids by Night)
Has hent him up aloof;
And full against the Beam he flung,
Where by the Back the Youth he hung
To spraul unneath the Roof.

From thence, 'Reverse my Charm, he crys,
'And let it fairely now suffice
'The Gambol has been shown.
But Oberon answers with a Smile,
Content thee Edwin for a while,
The Vantage is thine own.

Here ended all the Phantome-play;
They smelt the fresh Approach of Day,
And heard a Cock to crow;
The whirling Wind that bore the Crowd
Has clap'd the Door, and whistled loud,
To warn them all to go.

Then screaming all at once they fly,
And all at once the Tapers dy;
Poor Edwin falls to Floor;
Forlorn his State, and dark the Place,
Was never Wight in sike a Case
Through all the Land before.

But soon as Dan Apollo rose,
Full Jolly Creature home he goes,
He feels his Back the less;
His honest Tongue and steady Mind
Han rid him of the Lump behind
Which made him want Success.
With lusty livelyhed he talks,
He seems a dauncing as he walks,
His Story soon took wind;
And beautious Edith sees the Youth,
Endow'd with Courage, Sense and Truth,
Without a Bunch behind.
The Story told, Sir Topaz mov'd,
(The Youth of Edith erst approv'd)
To see the Revel Scene:
At close of Eve he leaves his home,
And wends to find the ruin'd Dome
All on the gloomy Plain.
As there he bides, it so befell,
The Wind came rustling down a Dell,
A shaking seiz'd the Wall:
Up spring the Tapers as before,
The Faeries bragly foot the Floor,
And Musick fills the Hall.
But certes sorely sunk with woe
Sir Topaz sees the Elphin show,
His Spirits in him dy:
When Oberon crys, 'a Man is near,
'A mortall Passion, cleeped Fear,
'Hangs flagging in the Sky.
With that Sir Topaz (Hapless Youth!)
In Accents fault'ring ay for Ruth
Intreats them Pity graunt;
For als he been a mister Wight
Betray'd by wand'ring in the Night
To tread the circled Haunt;
'Ah Losell Vile, at once they roar!
'And little skill'd of Faerie lore,
'Thy Cause to come we know:
'Now has thy Kestrell Courage fell;
'And Faeries, since a Ly you tell,
'Are free to work thee Woe.
Then Will, who bears the wispy Fire
To trail the Swains among the Mire,
The Caitive upward flung;
There like a Tortoise in a Shop
He dangled from the Chamber-top,
Where whilome Edwin hung.
The Revel now proceeds apace,
Deffly they frisk it o'er the Place,
They sit, they drink, and eat;

The time with frolick Mirth beguile,
And poor Sir Topaz hangs the while
'Till all the Rout retreat.
By this the Starrs began to wink,
They skriek, they fly, the Tapers sink,
And down ydrops the Knight.
For never Spell by Faerie laid
With strong Enchantment bound a Glade
Beyond the length of Night.
Chill, dark, alone, adreed, he lay,
'Till up the Welkin rose the Day,
Then deem'd the Dole was o'er:
But wot ye well his harder Lot?
His seely Back the Bunch has got
Which Edwin lost afore.
This Tale a Sybil-Nurse ared;
She softly strok'd my youngling Head,
And when the Tale was done,
'Thus some are born, my Son (she cries)
'With base Impediments to rise,
'And some are born with none.
'But Virtue can it self advance
'To what the Fav'rite Fools of Chance
'By Fortune seem'd design'd;
'Virtue can gain the Odds of Fate,
'And from it self shake off the Weight
'Upon th' unworthy Mind.

The Third Satire of Dr John Donne

Compassion checks my spleen, yet Scorn denies
The tears a passage thro' my swelling eyes;
To laugh or weep at sins, might idly show,
Unheedful passion, or unfruitful woe.
Satyr! arise, and try thy sharper ways,
If ever Satyr cur'd an old disease.

Is not Religion (Heav'n-descended dame)
As worthy all our soul's devoutest flame,
As Moral Virtue in her early sway,
When the best Heathens saw by doubtful day?
Are not the joys, the promis'd joys above,
As great and strong to vanquish earthly love,
As earthly glory, fame, respect and show,
As all rewards their virtue found below?
Alas! Religion proper means prepares,
These means are ours, and must its End be theirs?
And shall thy Father's spirit meet the sight
Of Heathen Sages cloath'd in heavenly light,

Whose Merit of strict life, severely suited
To Reason's dictates, may be faith imputed?
Whilst thou, to whom he taught the nearer road,
Art ever banish'd from the bless'd abode.

Oh! if thy temper such a fear can find,
This fear were valour of the noblest kind.

Dar'st thou provoke, when rebel souls aspire,
Thy Maker's Vengeance, and thy Monarch's Ire?
Or live entomb'd in ships, thy leader's prey,
Spoil of the war, the famine, or the sea?
In search of pearl, in depth of ocean breathe,
Or live, exil'd the sun, in mines beneath?
Or, where in tempests icy mountains roll,
Attempt a passage by the Northern pole?
Or dar'st thou parch within the fires of Spain,
Or burn beneath the line, for Indian gain?
Or for some Idol of thy Fancy draw,
Some loose-gown'd dame; O courage made of straw!
Thus, desp'rate Coward! would'st thou bold appear,
Yet when thy God has plac'd thee Centry here,
To thy own foes, to his, ignobly yield,
And leave, for wars forbid, the appointed field?

Know thy own foes; th' Apostate Angel, he
You strive to please, the foremost of the Three;
He makes the pleasures of his realm the bait,
But can he give for Love, that acts in Hate?
The World's thy second Love, thy second Foe,
The World, whose beauties perish as they blow,
They fly, she fades herself, and at the best
You grasp a wither'd strumpet to your breast.
The Flesh is next, which in fruition wasts,
High flush'd with all the sensual joys it tasts,
While men the fair, the goodly Soul destroy,
From whence the flesh has pow'r to tast a joy.

Seek thou Religion, primitively sound
Well, gentle friend, but where may she be found?

By Faith Implicite blind Ignaro led,
Thinks the bright Seraph from his Country fled,
And seeks her seat at Rome, because we know
She there was seen a thousand years ago;
And loves her Relick rags, as men obey
The foot-cloth where the Prince sat yesterday.

These pageant Forms are whining Obed's scorn,
Who seeks Religion at Geneva born,
A sullen thing, whose coarsness suits the crowd,

Tho' young, unhandsome; tho' unhandsome, proud:
Thus, with the wanton, some perversely judge
All girls unhealthy but the Country drudge.

No foreign schemes make easy Cæpio roam,
The man contented takes his Church at home;
Nay should some Preachers, servile bawds of gain,
Shou'd some new Laws, which like new-fashions reign,
Command his faith to count Salvation ty'd
To visit his, and visit none beside,
He grants Salvation centers in his own,
And grants it centers but in his alone:
From youth to age he grasps the proffer'd dame,
And they confer his Faith, who give his Name:
So from the Guardian's hands, the Wards who live
Enthral'd to Guardians, take the wives they give.

From all professions careless Airy flies,
For, all professions can't be good, he cries,
And here a fault, and there another views,
And lives unfix'd for want to heart to chuse:
So men, who know what some loose girls have done,
For fear of marrying such, will marry none.

The Charms of all, obsequious Courtly strike;
On each he doats, on each attends alike;
And thinks, as diff'rent countrys deck the dame,
The dresses altering, and the sex the same;
So fares Religion, chang'd in outward show,
But 'tis Religion still, where'er we go:
This blindness springs from an excess of light,
And men embrace the wrong to chuse the right.

But thou of force must one Religion own,
And only one, and that the Right alone.
To find that Right one, ask thy Reverend Sire;
Let him of his, and him of his enquire;
Tho' Truth and Falshood seem as twins ally'd,
There's Eldership on Truth's delightful side,
Her seek with heed—who seeks the soundest First
Is not of No Religion, nor the worst.
T' adore, or scorn an Image, or protest,
May all be bad: doubt wisely for the best;
'Twere wrong to sleep, or headlong run astray;
It is not wandring, to inquire the way.

On a large mountain, at the Basis wide,
Steep to the top, and craggy at the side,
Sits sacred Truth enthron'd; and he, who means
To reach the summit, mounts with weary pains,
Winds round and round, and every turn essays

Where sudden breaks resist the shorter ways.

Yet labour so, that, e're faint age arrive,
Thy searching soul possess her Rest alive;
To work by twilight were to work too late,
And Age is twilight to the night of fate.
To will implyes delay, therefore now do:
Hard deeds, the bodie's pain; hard knowledge too
The mind's indeavours reach; and mysteries
Are like the Sun dazling, yet plain to all eyes.
Keep the truth thou hast found; men do not stand
In so ill case, that God hath with his hand
Sign'd Kings blank-charters to kill whom they hate,
Nor are they Vicars, but hangmen to Fate.
Fool and wretch, wilt thou let thy soul be tyed
To mans laws, by which she shall not be tryed
At the last day? Or will it then boot thee
To say a Philip or a Gregory,
A Harry or a Martin taught me this?
Is not this excuse for meer contraries,
Equally strong, cannot both sides say so?
That thou mayest rightly obey power, her bounds know;
Those past, her nature, and name are chang'd; to be
Then humble to her is Idolatry.
As streams are, Power is; those blest flowers that dwell
At the rough streams calm head, thrive and do well,
But having left their roots, and themselves given
To the streams tyrannous rage, alas, are driven
Through Mills, Rocks, and Woods, and at last, almost
Consum'd in going, in the sea are lost:
So perish Souls, which more chuse mens unjust
Power, from God claim'd, then God himself to trust.
To will alone, is but to mean delay;
To work at present is the use of day:
For man's employ much thought and deed remain,
High Thoughts the Soul, hard deeds the body strain:
And Myst'ries ask believing, which to View
Like the fair Sun, are plain, but dazling too.

Be Truth, so found, with sacred heed possest,
Not Kings have pow'r to tear it from thy breast,
By no blank Charters harm they where they hate,
Nor are they Vicars, but the hands of Fate.
Ah! fool and wretch, who let'st thy soul be ty'd
To human Laws! Or must it so be try'd?
Or will it boot thee, at the latest day,
When Judgment sits, and Justice asks thy plea,
That Philip that, or Greg'ry taught thee this,
Or John or Martin? All may teach amiss:
For, every contrary in each Extream
This holds alike, and each may plead the same.

Wou'dst thou to Pow'r a proper duty shew?
'Tis thy first task the bounds of pow'r to know;
The bounds once past, it holds the name no more,
Its nature alters, which it own'd before,
Nor were submission humbleness exprest,
But all a low Idolatry at best.

Pow'r, from above subordinately spread,
Streams like a fountain from th' eternal head;
There, calm and pure the living waters flow,
But roar a Torrent or a Flood below;
Each flow'r, ordain'd the Margins to adorn,
Each native Beauty, from its roots is torn,
And left on Deserts, Rocks and Sands, or tost
All the long travel, and in Ocean lost:
So fares the soul, which more that Pow'r reveres
Man claims from God, than what in God inheres.

On the Number Three

Beauty rests not in one fix'd Place,
But seems to reign in every Face;
'Tis nothing sure, but Fancy then,
In various Forms bewitching Men;
Or is it Shape and Colour fram'd,
Proportion just, and woman nam'd?
If Fancy only rul'd in Love,
Why shou'd it then so strongly move?
Or why shou'd all that Look, agree
To own its mighty Pow'r in three?
In Three it shews a different Face,
Each shining with peculiar Grace;
Kindred a Native Likeness gives,
Which pleases, as in All it lives;
And where the Features disagree,
We praise the dear Variety.
Then Beauty surely ne'er was yet,
So much unlike it self and so complete.

A Hymn for Noon

The sun is swiftly mounted high;
It glitters in the southern sky;
Its beams with force and glory beat,
And fruitful earth is fill'd with heat.
Father, also with Thy fire

Warm the cold, the dead desire,
And make the sacred love of Thee
Within my soul a sun to me.
Let it shine so fairly bright
That nothing else be took for light,
That worldly charms be seen to fade,
And in its lustre find a shade.
Let it strongly shine within
To scatter all the clouds of sin,
That drive when gusts of passion rise
And intercept it from our eyes.
Let its glory more than vie
With the sun that lights the sky;
Let it swiftly mount in air,
Mount with that, and leave it there,
And soar with more aspiring flight
To realms of everlasting light.
Thus, while here I'm forc'd to be,
I daily wish to live with Thee,
And feel that union which Thy love
Will, after death, complete above.
From my soul I send my prayer;
Great creator, bow Thine ear;
Thou for whose propitious sway
The world was taught to see the day,
Who spake the word and earth begun
And show'd its beauties in the sun;
With pleasure I Thy creatures view,
And would with good affection, too,
Good affection sweetly free,
Loose from them and move to Thee;
O teach me due returns to give,
And to Thy glory let me live,
And then my days shall shine the more
Or pass more blessed than before.

A Hymn for Evening

The beam-repelling mists arise,
And evening spreads obscurer skies;
The twilight will the night forerun,
And night itself be soon begun.
Upon thy knees devoutly bow,
And pray the Lord of glory now
To fill thy breast, or deadly sin
May cause a blinder night within.
And whether pleasing vapours rise
Which gently dim the closing eyes,
Which make the weary members bless'd

With sweet refreshment in their rest,
Or whether spirits in the brain
Dispel their soft embrace again,
And on my watchful bed I stay,
Forsook by sleep and waiting day,
Be God for ever in my view
And never He forsake me, too;
But, still as day concludes in night
To break again with new-born light,
His wondrous bounty let me find
With still a more enlighten'd mind
When grace and love in one agree,
Grace from God, and love from me,
Grace that will from heaven inspire,
Love that seals it with desire,
Grace and love that mingle beams,
And fill me with encreasing flames.
Thou that hast Thy palace far
Above the moon and every star,
Thou that sittest on a throne
To which the night was never known,
Regard my voice and make me bless'd,
By kindly granting its request.
If thoughts on Thee my soul employ,
My darkness will afford me joy,
'Till Thou shalt call, and I shall soar,
And part with darkness evermore.

A Hymn for Morning

See the star that leads the day
Rising shoots a golden ray,
To make the shades of darkness go
From heaven above and earth below;
And warn us early with the sight
To leave the beds of silent night,
From a heart sincere and sound
From its very deepest ground,
Send devotion up on high
Wing'd with heat to reach the sky.
See the time for sleep has run,
Rise before, or with the sun,
Lift thine hands and humbly pray
The fountain of eternal day,
That as the light serenely fair
Illustrates all the tracts of air,
The sacred spirit so may rest
With quick'ning beams upon thy breast,
And kindly clean it all within

From darker blemishes of sin,
And shine with grace until we view
The realm it gilds with glory, too.
See the day that dawns in air,
Brings along its toil and care;
From the lap of night it springs
With heaps of business on its wings;
Prepare to meet them in a mind
That bows submissively resign'd,
That would to works appointed fall,
And knows that God has order'd all.
And whether with a small repast
We break our sober morning fast,
Or in our thoughts and houses lay
The future methods of the day,
Or early walk abroad to meet
Our business, with industrious feet,
Whate'er we think, whate'er we do,
His glory still be kept in view.
O Giver of eternal bliss,
Heavenly Father, grant me this;
Grant it all as well as me,
All whose hearts are fix'd on Thee,
Who revere Thy Son above,
Who Thy sacred Spirit love.

Piety, or, The Vision

'Twas when the night in silent sable fled,
When chearful morning sprung with rising red,
When dreams and vapours leave to crowd the brain,
And best the Vision draws its heav'nly scene;
'Twas then, as slumb'ring on my couch I lay,
A sudden splendor seem'd to kindle day,
A breeze came breathing in a sweet perfume,
Blown from eternal gardens, fill'd the room;
And in a void of blue, that clouds invest,
Appear'd a daughter of the realms of rest;
Her head a ring of golden glory wore,
Her honour'd hand the sacred volume bore,
Her rayment glitt'ring seem'd a silver white,
And all her sweet companions sons of light.

Strait as I gaz'd my fear and wonder grew,
Fear barr'd my voice, and wonder fix'd my view,
When lo! a cherub of the shining crowd
That sail'd as guardians in her azure cloud,
Fann'd the soft air and downward seem'd to glide,
And to my lips a living coal applied;

Then while the warmth on all my pulses ran,
Diffusing comfort, thus the maid began.

'Where glorious mansions are prepar'd above,
'The seats of Music, and the seats of Love,
'Thence I descend, and piety my name,
'To warm thy bosom with celestial flame,
'To teach thee praises mix'd with humble pray'rs,
'And tune thy soul to sing seraphic airs;
'Be thou my bard.' A vial here she caught,
(An angel's hand the chrystal vial brought)
And as with awful sound the word was said,
She pour'd a sacred unction on my head,
Then thus proceeded. 'Be thy muse thy zeal,
'Dare to be good, and all my joys reveal;
'While other pencils flatt'ring forms create,
'And paint the gawdy plumes that deck the great;
'While other pens exalt the vain delight,
'Whose wasteful revel wakes the depth of night;
'Or others softly sing in idle lines,
'How Damon courts, or Amaryllis shines;
'More wisely thou select a theme divine;
''Tis Fame's their recompence, 'tis Heav'n is thine.

'Despise the fervours of unhallow'd fire,
'Where wine, or passion, or applause inspire,
'Low restless life, and ravings born of earth,
'Whose meaner subjects speak their humble birth;
'Like working seas, that when loud Winters blow,
'Not made for rising, only rage below:
'Mine is a great, and yet a lasting heat,
'More lasting still, as more intensely great,
'Produc'd where pray'r, and praise, and pleasure breathe,
'And ever mounting whence it shot beneath.

'Unpaint the Love that hov'ring over beds,
'From glitt'ring pinions guilty pleasure sheds,
'Restore the colour to the golden mines
'With which behind the feather'd idol shines;
'To flow'ring greens give back their native care,
'The rose and lily never his to wear;
'To sweet Arabia send the balmy breath,
'Strip the fair flesh, and call the phantom Death;
'His bow be sabled o'er, his shafts the same,
'And fork and point them with eternal flame.

'But urge thy pow'rs, thine utmost voice advance,
'Make the loud strings against thy fingers dance,
''Tis Love that angels praise, and men adore,
''Tis Love Divine that asks it all and more:
'Fling back the gates of ever-blazing day,

'Pour floods of liquid light to gild the way,
'And all in glory wrapt, thro' paths untrod,
'Pursue the great unseen descent of GOD!
'Hail the meek virgin, bid the child appear,
'The child is GOD! and call him Jesus here;
'He comes; but where to rest? a manger's nigh,
'Make the great being in a manger lye;
'Fill the wide skies with angels on the wing,
'Make thousands gaze, and make ten thousand sing:
'Let men afflict him, men he came to save,
'And still afflict him, 'till he reach the grave;
'Make him resign'd, his loads of sorrow meet,
'And me, like Mary, weep beneath his feet;
'I'll bathe my tresses there, my pray'rs rehearse,
'And glide in flames of love along thy verse.

'Hah! while I speak, I feel my bosom swell,
'My raptures smother what I long to tell!
''Tis GOD! a present GOD! thro' cleaving air
'I see the throne! I see the Jesus there!
'Plac'd on the right; he shows the wounds he bore!
'(My fervours oft have won him thus before)
'How pleas'd he looks! my words have reach'd his ear,
'He bids the gates unbar, and calls me near.'

She ceas'd. The cloud on which she seem'd to tread,
Its curls unfolded, and around her spread;
Bright angels waft their wings to raise the cloud,
And sweep their iv'ry lutes, and sing aloud;
The scene moves off, while all its ambient sky
Is tun'd to wond'rous music, as they fly;
And soft the swelling sounds of music grow,
And faint their softness, till they fail below.

My downy sleep the warmth of Phoebus broke,
And while my thoughts were settling, thus I spoke;
Thou beauteous Vision on the soul imprest,
When most my reason wou'd appear to rest!
'Twas sure with pencils dipt in various lights
Some curious angel limn'd thy sacred sights;
From blazing suns his radiant gold he drew,
White moons the silver gave, and air the blue.
I'll mount the roving wind's expanded wing,
And seek the sacred hill, and light to sing;
('Tis known in Jewry well) I'll make my lays,
Obedient to thy summons, sound with praise.

But still I fear, unwarm'd with holy flame,
I take for truth the flatt'ries of a dream;
And barely wish the wond'rous gift I boast,
And faintly practise what deserves it most.

'Indulgent lord! whose gracious love displays
Joys in the light, and fills the dark with ease;
Be this, to bless my days, no dream of bliss,
Or be, to bless my nights, my dreams like this.

Song – When They Beauty Appears

When thy beauty appears
In its graces and airs
All bright as an angel new dropp'd from the sky,
At distance I gaze and am awed by my fears:
So strangely you dazzle my eye!

But when without art
Your kind thoughts you impart,
When your love runs in blushes through every vein;
When it darts from your eyes, when it pants in your heart,
Then I know you're a woman again.

There 's a passion and pride
In our sex (she replied),
And thus, might I gratify both, I would do:
Still an angel appear to each lover beside,
But still be a woman to you.

After the French Manner

As Pope who gathers mony to translate
With Gay the Shepheard Writer mett of late.
Says Pope, your Ecclogues wont come out wth speed
For Phillips to reprieve him Tonson feed.
Indeed the story may be true, says Gay,
For Your Subscriptions give him powr to pay.

The Ectasy

The fleeting Joy that all things have beneath
Goes off like snow while Zephirs warmly breath
The happy wish that makes our bliss compleat
it is not wealth it is not to be great
To glide along on pleasures easy floud
Or in fames wreaths to shine above the croud
Weak man who charms in these alone can see
Hear what I ask & learn to ask of me.

Send to my breast Allmighty King send down
A beam of brightness from thy starry throne
Break on my mind drive errors cloud away
& make a calm in passions troubled sea
that the poor banishd Soul serene & free
May rise from earth to visit heav'n & thee.
Come peace Divine shed gently from above
Inspire my willing bosome wondrous love
& lend thy wings & teach me how to move

But Whither whither now? what wondrous fire
With this blest influence equalls my desire?
I rise or love the kind deluder reigns
& acts in fancy such inchanted scenes
The earth retires, the parting skyes give way
& now I view the native realms of day
I mount above the starrs above the sun
& still methinks the spirit bears me on.
O strange enjoyment of a bliss unseen!
O ravishment! o sacred rage within!
Tumultuous pleasure raisd on peace of mind
Which he thats good & onely he can find!
I hear (it must be so) Ime sure I hear
Seraphick musick strike my rapturd ear
I see the light that veiles the throne on high
A light too glorious for the dazzled eye
look how around this great mysterious place
The Angells fly & as they fly they praise
Look how Apostles prophets martyrs Joyn
& all their tongues & all their harps combine
to celebrate the Majesty divine
to please heav'ns King their heav'nly lays are sung
No voice is silent not a harp unstrung

Pure & immortall quire allow me now
Since faign my heart woud pay its tribute too
Allow my Zeal to bear a part wth you
Assist my words and as they move along
With Halelujah's crown the burthend song

Father Eternall, God of truth & light
Great above all beyond expression bright
No bounds thy knowledge none thy powr confine
For powr & knowledge in their source are thine
Around thee Glory spreads her golden wing
Sing Glittering Angells Halelujah sing.

Son of the Father, blest, begotten Son
Ere the short measuring line of time begun
In thee his perfect Essence makes abode

the world has seen thy workes & owns thee God
The world must own thee loves unfathomd spring.
Sing Glittering Angells Halelujah Sing.

Proceeding Spirit, Equally divine
In whom the Godheads true perfections shine
You fill our bosomes with celestiall fire
& tis a bliss to burn when you inspire
O Lord Of Grace for Grace on earth you bring.
sing glittering Angells Halelujah sing

But Ah whats this? & where is all my heat
What interruption makes my Joy retreat
the worlds gott in my meditation crost
& the gay pictures in my fancy lost
How willingly Alas our soules woud rise
& be fixd starrs inserted in the skyes
But our attempts these chains of earth restrain
Deride our toiles & dragg us down again
Thus meteors mounting with the planets vie
But their own bodys sink them in the Sky
When the warmths gon that taught ym how to fly.

The Convert's Love

Blessed Light of saints on high
Who fill the mansions of the sky,
Sure defence, whose mercy still
Preserves thy subjects here from ill,
O my Jesus! make me know
How to pay the thanks I owe.

As the fond sheep that id'ly strays
With wanton play thro' winding ways,
Which never hits the road of home,
O'er Wilds of danger learns to roam,
'Till weari'd out with idle fear
And passing there and turning here,
He will for rest to covert run
And meet the wolf he wish'd to shun;
Thus wretched I, thro' wanton will
Run blind and headlong on in ill:
'Twas thus from sin to sin I flew
And thus I might have perish'd too;
But mercy dropt the likeness here
And shew'd and sav'd me from my fear;
While o'er the darkness of my mind
The sacred spirit purely shin'd,
And mark'd and bright'ned all the way

Which leads to everlasting day,
And broke the thick'ning clouds of sin
And fix'd the light of love within.

From hence my ravish'd soul aspires
And dates the rise of its desires.
From hence to thee my God! I turn,
And fervent wishes say I burn,
I burn thy glorious face to see
And live in endless joy with thee.

There's no such ardent kind of flame
Between the lover and the dame,
Nor such affection parents bear
To their young and only heir,
Tho' join'd together both conspire
And boast a doubled force of fire.
My tender heart within its seat
Dissolves before the scorching heat,
As soft'ning wax is taught to run
Before the warmness of the sun.

O my flame my pleasing pain
Burn and purify my stain,
Warm me, burn me, day by day
'Till you purge my earth away,
'Till at the last I throughly shine
And turn a torch of love divine.

Satyr I. A Letter To A Friend. On Poets

Poets are bound by ye severest rules,
The great ones must be mad, ye little all are fools,
Thus wn. I rime 'tis at my own expence,
To please my friend, I drop my claim to sence.
But now ye greater sway wch custome bears,
To forfeit souls in oaths, or sence in verse?
The using of an ill has so much power,
Stamp it a fashion, & its ill no more.
Since then ye humour so extremely reigns,
That ye gay folly every brest unbends,
Let me beneath ye common shadow hide
The fault's not mine thats all ye worlds beside.
Say then if passion, discontent, or ease
Sho'd e're your friend wth poetry possess,
For these, and want, ye muses setters seeme,
To draw in cullies to their loosing game,
How may I know yepath I ought to tread,
For 'tis in all mens natures to succeed

Some one way more than any else beside.
Fancy the reigning planet of yer. mind
Guides poets, & like her they're unconfin'd;
A bounded genius will attempt to prove,
The stings of satyr, & ye flames of love,
Jear folly, virtue by example praise,
& move our passions & or. language raise
Happy one way but one he'l scorn to chuse
So much or. wilder hopes our parts abuse.
Durfy more luckily employs his quill
Weak as he is he knows his talent still.
Wn C---r taught how plays debaucht ye age
He left to V---ke to defend the stage,
In rufull ballad humbly pleas'd to rage.
How great & undisturb'd by censuring foes
Might eithers fame beneath thier wreaths repose
Had B---l nere written verse nor C---ve prose.
B---r in Epicks may be still inspir'd,
By men of sence approv'd by all ye rest admir'd
Let him of Williams thickned lawrells sing
While for himself from every page they spring
& that shall crowne ye poet wch adorns ye King
But nere to tread in scandalls rougher ways
Again depart ye peacefull realms of praise.
We read his satyr & his wit allow,
We read & own the blended malice too.
But oft his muse shows an unpointed tooth
Wn. a just turn of verse don't raise ye illnaturd truth
Low puns for wit his lines do often fill
& oft he rambles in too loose a stile;
The biting satyr fights in closer file.
Laborious T---te has many methods try'd,
To know wt. happy way he may succeed,
A play or two employ'd his hopes at first,
Far from ye best, a little from ye worst,
Then bits of foreign poets to or. tongue,
More happily he brought, more sweetly sung,
Flush'd with success, he rises up from hence,
To rescue David at his own expence.
So have I known some painters wn. a face
In spight of all their touches wants to please
Turn up its eys & alter all its dress
The auction piece a flowing glory wears,
& where the syren fail'd; ye saint appears.
Now I, who proudly authors thus arraign,
Am, may be, envious thought, & may be vain,
But if my lines can gain one friends esteem,
Or my diversion be, 'tis all my aim,
I never bid perhaps nere shall for fame.
Nay sho'd I find my censures too severe,
Ide in my changing prove my temper fair,

And see with joy an error disappear;
Let Dennis rules for writing well lay downe,
Believe wt he prescribes his play has done,
A preface write to shew he dos not faile,
Till Hypers to himself ye fop reveale.

Satyr II. To T:--- M.---Y. On Law

Health & advice an old acquaintance sends,
Health & advice, the wish & debt of friends,
Tis fitt I teach the templar how to thrive,
Who teaches me with temperance to live.
Be still then murmuring Clients for a while,
Ye noisy four Court walls awhile be still,
Splitt with hard banter, & the Lawyers tongue,
Now Give a gentler Eccho to my song.
Of Law I sing, inspire my weaker pen,
Lost Suits, & pleaders little usd to gain.

That angry Justice to her heaven went
There seems not so confessd an argument,
As Lawyers thriving in her name below,
When were she here again, again she'd go.
Thus courtiers, if a Kings from care wthdrawn,
Rise without meritt, & with fraud rule on.

All Law was conscience once, unmixd wth tricks,
Found out by interest, or for politicks:
To his award each happy village stands,
Whose awfull virtue most respect commands,
Nor bribes, nor favour swayd the rigid man,
But all his acts in golden order ran;
Till love of gain, or fame, found out ye croud,
& rose by seeming good, above the good.
From this gross error to relieve their lands
Projecting patriots gave their helping hands:
Then Laws were putt in writing, courts were reard,
& Men for forehead, & strong lungs preferrd,
A friend or whore became a heightning clause,
& mony grew the meritt of the cause.

Woud you be taught your paths of gain to tread,
But man wants little teaching to be bad,
Gett impudence, each nation has its share,
Or something which does wondrous like appear,
Scotch confidence, the vanity of France,
The surly English air, the Irish ignorance,
All stand for this, or up to this advance.
Letts hear the other side, the Judge commands,

& Tully rises with his brief in hand,
Tully so known, so little heard of late,
But bauling Matho wont give over yet,
Forbid & shameless still he quotes ye lawes
Till want of time & his unceasing noise,
Staves of a Judgement or obtains the cause.
Thus what the first of every term he gaines,
So great a family so well maintaines.
Poor modesty, as old records declare,
Was starvd to death behind the foremost barr.
Have many words, nor spare ye breath you sell,
Your Clients pleasd you labour, tho' you fail;
Hence fluent Nevolus his great success,
Smoothly he utters, finds his words with ease,
His reasons places in the clearest light,
& pleads with humour, where he has not right.
Livy, whose country talks upon his words,
Shows reason, reason if the cause affords,
& by his happy fault of speaking long
Makes some believe he shows it in ye wrong.
Your terms are too of wondrous consequence,
To dazzle ignorance, & puzzle sence.
& many private tricks besides are known,
Which practise finds, or custom has sett down.
Young Brutus, who so quickly came in play,
To gainfull fame found this effectuall way,
In formâ pauperis much he undertook,
As men who fish take worm upon ye hook,
& to be often heard, for nothing often spoke.
With this last rule I close my whole advice,
Take all you can, he looses who deny's,
Who by one side is usd may honest be,
But he is rich who takes of both his fee.
& least you want a story of your art,
Hear how began this double-dealing part.

In times of yore, & Æsops vocall grove,
When fingers talkd of something else then Love,
The hands fell out, the plaintiff, left maintaind,
The right in all things tho unjustly reignd.
Then this her plea, that had her answer heard,
This brought deponents, that Cross bills preferrd.
After a Long debate to make them pay,
(for you as well may hope to gett away,
for nought, as allmost nought) the Judges say,
What ere the world in other things intends,
To shew how much we wish relations friends,
As often as we can, the court decrees,
To use you both alike in taking fees

Satyr III. – On Virtue

Is virtue something reall here below
Or but an Idle name & empty show
While on this head I take my thoughts to task
Methinks young Freedom answers wt I ask
In his own moralls thus the Spark goes on
Or thus if he were here he might have don

In what wild hill or unfrequented plain
Hast thou been bred so ignorant of men
Such doubts in such a world to entertain
Or has thy father had an hopefull son
by Colledge education quite undon
& therefore wisely gave his others none
Believe me Sr that what you faign woud know
Is but a word to signify a show
Often it is 'tis often not designd
& still it makes a riddle of the mind.
Now see how evidently this appears
In the clear language of particulars.

All men do Sporus very chast esteem
But does he rule his will or nature him
What he might be himself he little knows
Who never had a passion to oppose
He must be chast with out a world of pains
For all his virtue is his impotence.

Damon the hottest rakell of the town
Has his cast misses on the common thrown
No signs of great repentance does he show
But the mans bound his wife's his virtue now

Nor friends nor glorious wine nor sparkling witt
Makes Codrus ere beyond a bottle sitt
This is his temperance his acquaintance say
& att the barr they give him leave to pay
But they forgett that Codrus is so poor
& all his virtue may be want of more

A sexton scarcely can resolve to ring
But Cotta flyes as on devotions wing
Tows his old aunt in black to every prayer
Whines as he goes & prayes aloud when there
Thus to be Guardian when she dies he'le gett
His virtue is the hopes of pow'r to cheat

Thus various mankind cou'd I quickly trace
& show how fondly we mistake their wayes

How something which they are not oft they seem
& how that something brings them in esteem
But to be short with in my self I feel
Too deeply rooted all the seeds of ill
Mad passions reason not invincible
& chance to be misguided in my will
Why shoud I think another has not these
Is he more perfect man or am I less.

To such a loose harangue on t'other side
My honest Trueman woud have thus replyd
While by yr own you blame anothers soul
You must go wrong & ye illbiassd bowl
Bear on a falser ground at every roul
Tis granted where the moralls run awry
There your reflections very justly ly
But think you there are none to good inclind
From the meer sway of reason on their mind
Think you that every one woud rather be
Slave to his passions then from passion free
For such they are who have no powr to stay
When every weak temptation calls away
Curio is summond to Corinna's house
Cross is his father cruell is her spouse
The dangers great but Curio must be gon
A pleasure tempts a passion hurry's on
Nor are the troubles which pursue it all
For you may feel the very fetters gall
Dispair & hope with lingring pangs remain
Sorrow & Joy give much a quicker pain
& love & hate in wild convulsions reign.
When with their proper objects these attack
Tis to be virtuous then to drive 'em back
Entrenchd with in ye rules wch prudence makes
Tis virtue still an æquall mind to bear
Nor swoln wth hope nor too depressed wth fear
To lett the Man secure from passion move
In reasons orb serenely plac'd above
Tis Virtue to maintain your country's cause
Support your king while he supports her laws
Nor in th' oppressing of a kingdom share
For fifteen hundred English pounds a year
Paid down by order of ye Commons here
Tis virtue & the highest mentiond yet
To think religion not a trick of state

Nature has fooles who know not of this way
& fooles alone have priviledge to stray
But if a Competence of Sense she give
& the receivers do not upright live
Their different failures do such words create

As Atheist traytor villain rakehell cheat
Defamer pander whore knight of ye post
& hypocrites a Common name for most
Most strive to varnish their prevailing vice
& grant with ease when they succeed in this
The Case the same where the appearance is
But goodness ever has the same appeard
While no design is still upon its guard
The best is onely but ye best begun
Sooner or later by its self undon

Ore peaceful citts the hectring bullys reign
But while they hector so they know their men
Shoud they vex one at last to Cudgells bred
The masque of valour wont protect ye head
While the tough cane insults the shining blade

I scorn in verity old Gripus cry's
This swearing this unprofitable vice
But mony mollifys the wretches scorn
& he who hates to swear will be forsworn

Thus ill men never fail of being known
How sly so e're a vizard they put on
But still the good both seem & are ye same
Unmovd by passion, int'rest, humour, fame
Tis thus that they deserve ye name of men
By ruling of themselves they empires gain
& laugh at fortune raisd above her reign.

Satyr IV. – The Pretty Gentleman

Where Creditors their bankrupt debtors stow
Where men for want of coin to durance go
& are for being wretched made more so
Where poor W---G---could months abide
When all his creditt would not him provide
With one nights lodging any where beside
There on a bed by moths half eat away
Damon ye witt ye generous ye gay
The heir of Eighteen hundred sterling lay
Sullen with grief impatient to endure
& yet oppressd with what he could not cure
Long did his thoughts upon his Sorrows dwell
Then they on generall reflections fell
For still the mind by private ills aggrievd
Is by the thought of common ills relieved
This soths ye spleen while that creates dispair
One you ingross in 'tother others share

Alass he crys how many have I known
By giddy pleasures & ymselves undon
We hunt for happiness on eager speed
& have a chance that we may all succeed
Reason & passion draw ye diffrent views
& we're all blessd according as we chuse
But to our reason seldom we attend
Tho' all our hopes upon that choice depend
See ye degrees thou heedless creature man
By which the passions on ye mind obtain
As in ye pretty Gentleman suppose
For instance how in him yr empire grows
Up from his swadling to his beauish clothes

Scarce can his tongue in tripping accents rove
But the nurse lulls him wth wild tales of love
Where a kings son as many such have been
Dyes for ye youngest daughter of a queen
These mold his temper till he learns to read
& then romantick authors fill his head
Where honour in enamelld armour bleeds
For love thats errant on ye milk white steed
How his eyes dance when magick Castles fly
When beautyes freed how pants his heart for Joy
How much what ere he reads he longs to try
When he can Nature more distinctly see
He finds such things as these coud never be
Yet still the prejudice is on his Soul
& love & honour must his actions rule
Then that he may their due proportions trace
Playes following nature he will follow playes
At these he dresses talkes fightes loves from these
He railes at buisness wch he does not know
Because ye poett who had none did so
In wine & whores & games his guinnys run
Because the like in such a part is don
Thats drawn with art to please ye lookers on
To repeat verse & with a grace be leud
Is gay is Dorimant & must be good
But when his fullgrown witt a figure makes
Without a guide agreably he rakes
Nor the stage longer for a pattern takes
Himself a mode a man of airs a beau
Nay poet too—as far as songs will go
Thus with a world of pains the work is past
& he's an entertaining fool at last
He does the men of buisness pitty move
The men of Moralls soberly reprove
The tradesmen cheat him—but the Ladies love.

As on this head he woud have spoken more
The Jailour happend to unlock the door
To lett him know his creditors did wait
To make him sell if he woud freedom gett
At least three quarters of his whole estate

Satyr V. Verse

Thou soft Engager of my tender years
Divertive verse now come & ease my cares
The Rake has wine the aged knave ye view
Of what his death bed Charity will do
To lay his cares & mine are layd by you
You give my mind when I unbend relief
Raise ev'ry Joy & lessen ev'ry grief
Nor do I onely these thy comforts find
Thy comforts are diffusive to mankind
The men of sense of buisness or of whims
Half witts or lovers ev'ry one sometimes
Will toy away a vacant hour in rimes

& they give all but lovers troubles ease
The Muses fires the flames of love encrease
Yet the fond fooles write more yn all ye rest
As if they studyd to be more unblest
Of Moving things they speak in moving strains
& moan & beg a cure of all their pains
Till at the last theyre workd to a belief
That what they said has been their reall grief
As strong as fate they call the chains they wear
To starrs & Angells ev'ry nymph compare
Then think their chains as strong, their nymphs as fair
Thus our loves more & more the womens pride
So the wounds deeper & the cure denyd
Long may you gentle souls your fetters wear
If still you write upon ye pangs you bear
Yet know that writing makes them more severe
If Celia or Aminta scornfull grow
On the great praises which your lines bestow
Long may you feel them since you make ym so

Verse is on other subjects less unkind
& with its transports brightens up ye mind
The Drunkards catch is half the rogues delight
Where noise & briskness do their charms unite
The drawers calld & ink & paper brought
& so extempore the work is wrought
While wine inspires they never stay for thought
The Jolly words are roard in tunefull sound

While the full bottles run the tables round
& Ecchoes from the Empty ones rebound
Raisd to the Joyes above the cares of kings
Their singing makes ym drink their drinking sing
O happy men if twere not for the curse
Of qualms repentance & an empty purse
But happy men at least for some few hours
Who force the Muse to nothing else but rime
& when your sense is drownd sing off yr time

Verse has another powr on other men
When the vexd thoughts by writing grow serene
Full of the spleen & rage & scorn to see
The tide of vice & folly run so high
Some from the world retire to poetry
& when their pens what grieves their bosoms speak
How honesty's a cully witt a rake
Fair Virtue beggerd beauty grown a baud
Religion made a masque & gold a God
Their breasts find ease by laying down their load
So Prophetts usd inspird of old to swell
& when they spoke their Oracles grew well

For me who never have a drinker been
Nor provd the witty forces of the spleen
For me who be it chance or carelessness
(forgive me half the world when I confess)
Have never been in love in all my dayes
On other principles my pen I take
For meer disintrested diversions sake
I onely write as many lovers woo
But just when I have nothing else to do
& then to please my self as well as you
I seek no praise & keep me safe from shame
Not known to many & unknown to fame
I woud not blunty rail a folly down
Nor with undecent rage on vices run
Our master Horace wisely sung of old
That satyrs better if it Jear then scold
The Gall too much prevailing spoils the ink
Nor woul I frett mankind but make ym think
Tis farr more human thus to show ye place
Where you ly open then throw in ye pass

Satyr VI. – The Spleen

Hail to the sacred silence of this Grove
Hail to the greens below the greens above
Oft have I found beneath these shady trees

A reall in imaginary bliss
For they my fancy sooth she's a cheat
Which can agreably adorn deceit
Some state of life she draws with pleasing art
Brings Enchanted reason to her part
Reason awhile is captive by consent
Acts from all its rigid rules unbent
From our own selves conceales our reall case
Nor shows us what may be but what may please
When I by these am from my self with drawn
I straight become what ere I think upon

Now do I turn a statesman of the rate
That furnishes the world beside with chat
I many use I make a friend of none
If I flatter tis my prince alone
Mankind well versd in various villany
Misrepresent each study'd Case to me
In long petitions a present fee
Sayes one your Lordship has ye royall ear
I some articles against me fear
For sinking publick funds in such a year
Then on my chair he layes a bag of coin
Nor dares to offer what he woud have mine
Another cryes I want a place at Court
Your Lships word woud make ye buisness short
I present two hundred guinnys for't
This as I take it is a life of state
When I think of this I think Ime great
But now a leaf is noisy by my head
My chain is broke all my greatness fled
In vain I woud recall the vanishd thought
Something I know did please I cant tell what
As I hunt the traces of my mind
In a new whim a new delight I find

Now among books my chief diversion lyes
I affect to be thought wondrous wise
In strange experiment discovery's
On All ye sorts shapes of flyes I read
Or print a book of shells as Lister did
When I meet a thing unknown till yn
I write for Holland to ye Learned men
The subtiltys of schooles with ease I cutt
Where learnings nothing but a meer dispute
With Ipse Dixit's fixd for arguments
Quibbles formd by rules hid with pains
Waging a warr of words in spight of sense
My skill in many languages is shown
Altho' I gracefully can speak in none
No Cares no business do my brain molest

The world admires the treasures of my breast
I in barren satisfaction rest

Here do I change Insensibly again
My gay fancy paints another scene
Heark or a pleasing madness charms my sense
Or I hear songs well tund instruments
Yes tis a ball where I with airs cloths
Engage the Ladys outshine the beaus
I chuse a creature beautious as the light
Of her I beg she denys a night
Scorn with the fair does still attendant go
They're proud because their outward charms they know
Fondly think them reasons to be so
But passion hearts of any temper moves
Anon shes complaisant anon she loves
When sated with the bliss their arms I quitt
I boast my triumph to each friend I meet
for men are now so scandalously vain
They think it less of pleasure to obtain
Their Joys then tell 'em or'e to other men
More of grief to hide the ripe amour
Then twas to smother infant love before
I drink I dance I swear I shake ye dice
Try each path of pleasurable vice
Till at ye last my wild unsettled life
Like Comedys is finishd in a wife

By Just degrees the breezes louder grow
The same breast they sooth they roughen too
Methinks Ime strangely alterd in a trice
All soft unmanly pleasures I despise
Warr is my buisness honour is my prize
I grasp it in my thoughts push along
Nor mind the toiles by which it must be won
With such bewitching powr the walking light
Leads men thro' all the dangers of the night
Ore hills vales they hunt the dazzling game
Nor feel the trouble while they see the flame
Strange force of Glory what a world are slain
To please the pride of two or three great men
How towns have fed on ratts yt scornd to yield
How dear ye hardy soldier buys ye field
Warm without anger to their arms they crowd
For anothers quarrell wast their blood
Some fight curse while others run pray
In Camps they rook each other at their play
Then the loosers mutIny for pay
Are my brave followers slain why lett ym dy
False musterd companys my purse supply
Thus summers fraud feeds winters luxury

When in warm quarters nature craves a punk
For the Queen I loyally get drunk

Give ore my wanton fancy now give ore
The clouds are gath'ring anon they'le powr
The pleasures of my groves are fled away
The sacred silence ye shiny day
What have you then to lull you in your play

Satyr VII. - The Isle Of Wight

In noble deeds our valiant fathers shone
We'le shine in all their glory's & our own
So Or---d does & O---d Leads us on

Thus say ye Gallant youth who bravely dare
Not to expect—tis more—to meet the warr

Ye Men of pleasure be like these, awake,
Your Country calls consider whats at stake
Our wealths decaying while our trading stands
& Europes Ballance shakes within our hands
This is a Cause thats greater nobler farr
Then wanton loves on beds of feathers are

Abroad your wounds meet plunder & renown
While infamy pursues your Jarrs in town
Where the whole acts a breach upon ye laws
perhaps a stew ye scene a **** ye cause

If here at home you stay & rack your brains
To find out fashions then to dress with pains
Vain is the humour, Idle the expence
The garb appears Phantastick which we see
Before 'tis grown familiar to the eye
& when it is then half its beauty's dy

If you would stay that Lady's shoud not want
A gay Mirtillo for a smooth Courant
Alas you need not speak to show your soul
Your bounds Coupees & sinks betray the fool
Men find a jest in evry diffrent step
For postures are the buisness of an ape

In short if you woud stay at home to run
Thro' all the lawless pleasures of the town
How vile the means how guilty is the end
How many troubles your designs attend
You live a life that merits infamy

& live to be forgotten when you dy

For shame arise & in this cause appear
It is not for our selves alone we're here
Your country Justly claims her share in you
& honour does her rightfull claim allow
Honour a courage still imployd in good
Unshockd by passions & above the croud
The soul in this Heroick beauty deckt
Stands over these triumphant & erect
Dares for its country any fate defy
& mounts a brave deserver of the sky

Some men of pleasure have been drawn so farr
By such like reasons as to think on warr
Straight in a heat their Horses they provide
& to the Ile of wight like warriors ride
Before them pistolls placd & swords aside
But with what arms the mock campaign is made
With inlaid pistolls & a guilded blade
Thus at a distance each the foe defy's
Who fears to meet a toil or leave a bliss
But for the ending of their great design
They light they see his grace in publick dine
They view the ships they talk among the men
& when a gale blows fair are gone again
The world believd they nobly did intend
Their Country by their going to defend
& now it wonders at the trifling end

Some Indians thus the town a gazing ore
Saw a white vizard hanging at a door
& wonderd at the fighting face it wore
But that soon turning with the change of wind
They wonderd more the counterfeit to find
So like a man before & nought behind.

Satyr IX. - The State Of Love Imitated Fm An Elegy Of Mons:r Desportes

In the st season of the infant earth
When all from Chaos took their orderd birth
When mankind from the hand of heaven came
All pure & white ere vice had gott a name
But evry act with innocence indu'd
Was more by nature then from knowledge good
Love mighty powr did graciously descend
grew fond of man & here wth man remaind
In their unsullyd hearts he chose to stay
their bliss anights their buisness all the day

Nor wonder if in such he made abode
No temples better can befitt a god
His gentle influence did their soules inspire
Each found a mate nor wanted amorous fire
Evn when injoyment had allayd desire
Secure of sweet content they daily livd
Content unmixd with fears to be deceivd
Their tongues their reall sentiments disclosd
Nor studyd language on the ears imposd
Their eyes an undissembling flame expresst
& they who felt it most coud speak it least
desert & softness love or beauty were
Their onely arts to make a yielding fair
Plain undesigning love that never knew
To practise crueltys as Empire grew
To fashion smiles with managd airs to court
& wound a tender breast in barb'rous sport
Twas more then riches riches coud not move
The meanest thought them not a price for love

But when the vices to a head increast
& all this age of downy pleasure ceast
When gold by glistring showd its dark abode
& fickleness began to be the mode
When feigning was by way of breeding taught
& onely worth his wealth the lover thought
When first to speak the mind was reckond shame
& masqd hypocrisy took honours name
The fatall change with anger Cupid saw
& thus bespoke ym ready to withdraw

Hence lett us hence with Just abhorrence go
For ill their happyness these mortalls know
Who slight the mighty favours I bestow

Then darting upwards soon ye clouds he gaind
& hung in air his purpose thus explaind

You shall repent ungratefull race you shall
& know too late the Joyes from whence you fall
The loss regretting by your selves undon
Who true contentments heavnly blisses shun
& after false appearing pleasures run
Since all in common do my Godhead slight
On all in common shall my fury light

& first on men who wont their hours employ
In my soft paths of simple artless Joy
Who woud be free tho for the worse you change
My powr shall thus my slighted gifts revenge
Henceforth your charmers shall be versd in arts

Not loving faithless & designing hearts
The tend'rest shall their pitty least obtain
They'le feel a pride ore many slaves to reign
To make believing fooles then give ym pain
Their look their smile their action their intent
Shall all against your peace of Soul be bent
Now hope restraining when it forward bears
Now quickning hope when you're restraind by fears
Oft seeming kind then scrupulously nice
& mixing as it were their flames with Ice
To keep confusd irresolute & rackt
Those bosoms they by various wayes distract
What pains you then shall feel wt rage express
How many purposes to love ym less
How many oaths to shun their sight you'le swear
Which never shall be kept against the fair
A tear a word thats feignd shall soon restore
Their empire & enslave their rebells more
No matter what you saw you must believe
For strange enchantments may the sight deceive

Nay more Ile change my quiver bow & darts
To make mad work within your alterd hearts
Nor ever give the pleasing wounds I usd
Ere you my empire scornd my laws refusd
Here one a nymph that is deformd shall fire
Another one to honour lost admire
& while all night by others she's embracd
The wretch shall doat because she acts the chast
Some shall be prodigall their end to gain
Nor know that who gives most shall least obtain
Their hopes will still be fed but never don
To keep them still in play & loving on
In short Ile make them feel & own it pain
To live beneath inconstant womans chain
& know their folly when they scornd my reign

& You ye women shall confess it too
Repenting that you ere from me withdrew
You who have given wealth its powr to move
& triumph ore the sacred rites of love
Who vice to virtue ignorance to parts
& mony can prefer to faithfull hearts
Who think to sell your selves is nothing mean
& from the prostituted bed reap gain
You never never shall again perceive
Rhe wondrous sweets that mutuall passions have
But for their mighty riches love the greal
While even they shall win you by deceit
Their purpose in inveagling flattrys hide
& the lost creatures whom they gain deride

Then leaving those that can be new no more
The self same arts to others practise ore
By such poor victorys to boast adress
& the faint glorys of their fame increase

As Huntsmen when they have a hare in view
Fird & impatient eagerly pursue
Now ore the mountains now across the plains
& for a little take a world of pains
Unweari'd still they follow with delight
Fond of the hunting tho the game they slight
Just so the great their amorous chace shall run
Nor ought to gain you shall be left undon
With oaths & sighs & tears they will assail
But love no more when ever these prevail
Unmindfull then of what had causd their cares
For other beautys they display their snares

While you who soon perceive their broken faith
Their oaths no more esteemd then common breath
Tho never by my flame divine inspird
Shall inly with a rage of soul be fird
All spight to find your flatterd charms contemnd
& mad to see another more esteemd
For Justly thus my anger does ordain
That you shoud each create ye others pain

When Cupid thus had spoke his wings he spread
& with redoubled springs to heaven fled
Nor were in Idle air his curses lost
Succeeding ages found them to their cost

Ah Madam you alas have found them true
The prophesy is made too good on you
You've had the great become your beautys slave
& by experience know the great deceive
& tho' those starrs of love your charming eyes
Outshine the brightness of the midday skys
Tho' your complexion with the morning vies
Tho all the Graces which around you wait
Dwell on each part & fill up beautys state
Tho the bright virtues which within remain
Might promise you an everlasting reign
You see the heart was givn to you before
At a new shrine anothers charms adore
But cease my lovely weeper ceáse to mourn
The fair that triumphs now will have her turn
No charm against inconstancy secures
You know the lovers fire but short endures
& she'le forsaken meet a fate like yours

The Book Worm

Come hither, Boy, we'll hunt to Day
The Book-Worm, ravening Beast of Prey,
Produc'd by Parent Earth, at odds
(As Fame reports it) with the Gods.
Him frantick Hunger wildly drives
Against a thousand Authors Lives:
Thro' all the Fields of Wit he flies;
Dreadful his Head with clust'ring Eyes,
With Horns without, and Tusks within,
And Scales to serve him for a Skin.
Observe him nearly, lest he climb
To wound the Bards of antient Time,
Or down the Vale of Fancy go
To tear some modern Wretch below:
On ev'ry Corner fix thine Eye,
Or ten to one he slips thee by.

See where his Teeth a Passage eat:
We'll rouse him from the deep Retreat.
But who the Shelter's forc'd to give?
'Tis Sacred Virgil as I live!
From Leaf to Leaf, from Song to Song,
He draws the tadpole Form along,
He mounts the gilded Edge before,
He's up, he scuds the Cover o'er,
He turns, he doubles, there he past,
And here we have him, caught at last.

Insatiate Brute, whose Teeth abuse
The sweetest Servants of the Muse.
(Nay never offer to deny,
I took thee in the Fact to fly.)
His Roses nipt in ev'ry Page,
My poor Anacreon mourns thy Rage.
By thee my Ovid wounded lies;
By thee my Lesbia's Sparrow dies:
Thy rabid Teeth have half destroy'd
The Work of Love in Biddy Floyd,
They rent Belinda's Locks away,
And spoil'd the Blouzelind of Gay.
For all, for ev'ry single Deed,
Relentless Justice bids thee bleed.
Then fall a Victim to the Nine,
My self the Priest, my Desk the Shrine.

Bring Homer, Virgil, Tasso near,
To pile a sacred Altar here;

Hold, Boy, thy Hand out-run thy Wit,
You reach'd the Plays that D---s writ;
You reach'd me Ph---s rustick Strain;
Pray take your mortal Bards again.

Come bind the Victim,—there he lies,
And here between his num'rous Eyes
This venerable Dust I lay,
From Manuscripts just swept away.

The Goblet in my Hand I take,
(For the Libation's yet to make)
A Health to Poets! all their Days
May they have Bread, as well as Praise;
Sense may they seek, and less engage
In Papers fill'd with Party-Rage.
But if their Riches spoil their Vein
Ye Muses, make them poor again.

Now bring the Weapon, yonder Blade,
With which my tuneful Pens are made.
I strike the Scales that arm thee round,
And twice and thrice I print the Wound;
The sacred Altar floats with red,
And now he dies, and now he's dead.

How like the Son of Jove I stand,
This Hydra stretch'd beneath my Hand!
Lay bare the Monster's Entrails here,
To see what Dangers threat the Year:
Ye Gods! what Sonnets on a Wench?
What lean Translations out of French?
'Tis plain, this Lobe is so unsound,
S--- prints, before the Months go round.

But hold, before I close the Scene,
The sacred Altar shou'd be clean.
Oh had I Sh---ll's Second Bays,
Or T---! thy pert and humble Lays!
(Ye Pair, forgive me, when I vow
I never miss'd your Works till now)
I'd tear the Leaves to wipe the Shrine,
(That only way you please the Nine)
But since I chance to want these two,
I'll make the Songs of D---y do.

Rent from the Corps, on yonder Pin,
I hang the Scales that brac't it in;
I hang my studious Morning Gown,
And write my own Inscription down.

'This Trophy from the Python won,
'This Robe, in which the Deed was done,
'These, Parnell glorying in the Feat,
'Hung on these Shelves, the Muses Seat.
'Here Ignorance and Hunger found
'Large Realms of Wit to ravage round;
'Here Ignorance and Hunger fell;
'Two Foes in one I sent to Hell.
'Ye Poets, who my Labours see,
'Come share the Triumph all with me!
'Ye Criticks! born to vex the Muse,
'Go mourn the grand Ally you lose.

An Impromptu Like Martial

Gays gon out early, how comes it to pass?
Not that he has buisness, but thinks that he has

Song – My Days Have Have Been So Wondrous Free

My days have been so wondrous free,
The little birds that fly
With careless ease from tree to tree,
Were but as bless'd as I.

Ask gliding waters, if a tear
Of mine increas'd their stream?
Or ask the flying gales, if e'er
I lent one sigh to them?

But now my former days retire,
And I'm by beauty caught;
The tender chains of sweet desire
Are fix'd upon my thought.

Ye nightingales, ye twisting pines!
Ye swains that haunt the grove!
Ye gentle echoes, breezy winds!
Ye close retreats of love!

With all of nature, all of art,
Assist the dear design;
Oh teach a young, unpractic'd heart
To make my Nancy mine!

The very thought of change I hate,
As much as of despair;

Nor ever covet to be great,
Unless it be for her.

'Tis true, the passion in my mind
Is mix'd with soft distress;
Yet while the fair I love is kind,
I cannot wish it less.

The Vigil of Venus

Let those love now, who never lov'd before,
Let those who always lov'd, now love the more.

The Spring, the new, the warb'ling Spring appears,
The youthful Season of reviving Years;
In Spring the Loves enkindle mutual Heats,
The feather'd Nation chuse their tuneful Mates,
The Trees grow fruitful with descending Rain
And drest in diff'ring Greens adorn the Plain.
She comes; to morrow Beauty's Empress roves
Thro' Walks that winding run within the Groves;
She twines the shooting Myrtle into Bow'rs,
And ties their meeting Tops with Wreaths of Flow'rs,
Then rais'd sublimely on her easy Throne
From Nature's pow'rful Dictates draws her own.
Let those love now, who never lov'd before,
Let those who always lov'd, now love the more.

'Twas on that Day which saw the teeming Flood
Swell round, impregnate with celestial Blood;
Wand'ring in Circles stood the finny Crew,
The midst was left a void Expanse of Blue,
There Parent Ocean work'd with heaving Throes,
And dropping wet the fair Dione rose.
Let those love now, who never lov'd before,
Let those who always lov'd, now love the more.

She paints the purple Year with vary'd show,
Tips the green Gem, and makes the Blossom glow.
She makes the turgid Buds receive the Breeze,
Expand to Leaves, and shade the naked Trees.
When gath'ring damps the misty Nights diffuse,
She sprinkles all the Morn with balmy Dews;
Bright trembling Pearls depend at ev'ry spray,
And kept from falling, seem to fall away.
A glossy Freshness hence the Rose receives,
And blushes sweet through all her silken Leaves;
(The Drops descending through the silent Night,
While Stars serenely roll their golden Light,)

Close 'till the Morn, her humid Veil she holds;
Then deckt with Virgin Pomp the Flow'r unfolds.
Soon will the Morning blush: Ye Maids! prepare,
In rosy Garlands bind your flowing Hair
'Tis Venus' Plant: The Blood fair Venus shed,
O'er the gay Beauty pour'd immortal Red;
From Love's soft Kiss a sweet Ambrosial Smell
Was taught for ever on the Leaves to dwell;
From Gemms, from Flames, from orient Rays of Light
The richest Lustre makes her Purple bright;
And she to morrow weds; the sporting Gale
Unties her Zone, she bursts the verdant Veil;
Thro' all her Sweets the rifling Lover flies,
And as he breaths, her glowing Fires arise.
Let those love now, who never lov'd before,
Let those who always lov'd, now love the more.

Now fair Dione to the Myrtle Grove
Sends the gay Nymphs, and sends her tender Love.
And shall they venture? is it safe to go?
While Nymphs have Hearts, and Cupid wears a Bow?
Yes safely venture, 'tis his Mother's Will;
He walks unarm'd and undesigning ill,
His Torch extinct, his Quiver useless hung,
His Arrows idle, and his Bow unstrung.
And yet, ye Nymphs, beware, his Eyes have Charms,
And Love that's naked, still is Love in Arms.
Let those love now, who never lov'd before,
Let those who always lov'd, now love the more.

From Venus Bow'r to Delia's Lodge repairs
A Virgin Train compleat with modest Airs:
'Chast Delia! grant our Suit! or shun the Wood,
'Nor stain this sacred Lawn with savage Blood.
'Venis, O Delia! if she cou'd persuade,
'Wou'd ask thy Presence, might she ask a Maid.
Here chearful Quires for three auspicious Nights
With Songs prolong the pleasurable Rites:
Here Crouds in Measures lightly-decent rove;
Or seek by Pairs the Covert of the Grove,
Where meeting Greens for Arbours arch above,
And mingling Flowrets strow the Scenes of Love.
Here dancing Ceres shakes her golden Sheaves:
Here Bacchus revels, deckt with viny Leaves:
Here Wit's enchanting God in Lawrel crown'd
Wakes all the ravish'd Hours with silver Sound.
Ye Fields, ye Forests, own Dione's Reign,
And Delia, Huntress Della, shun the Plain.
Let those love now, who never lov'd before,
Let those who always lov'd, now love the more.

Gay with the Bloom of all her opening Year,
The Queen at Hybla bids her Throne appear;
And there presides; and there the fav'rite Band
(Her smiling Graces) share the great Command.
Now beauteous Hybla! dress thy flow'ry Beds
With all the Pride the lavish Season sheds,
Now all thy Colours, all thy Fragrance yield,
And rival Enna's Aromatick Field.
To fill the Presence of the gentle Court
From ev'ry Quarter rural Nymphs resort,
From Woods, from Mountains, from their humble Vales,
From Waters curling with the wanton Gales.
Pleas'd with the joyful Train, the laughing Queen
In Circles seats them round the Bank of green;
And 'lovely Girls, (she whispers) guard your Hearts;
'My Boy, tho' stript of Arms, abounds in Arts.
Let those love now, who never lov'd before,
Let those who always lov'd, now love the more.

Let tender Grass in shaded Allys spread,
Let early Flow'rs erect their painted Head.
To morrow's Glory be to morrow seen,
That Day, old Ether wedded Earth in green.
The Vernal Father bid the Spring appear,
In Clouds he coupled to produce the Year,
The Sap descending o'er her Bosom ran,
And all the various sorts of Soul began.
By Wheels unknown to Sight, by secret Veins
Distilling Life, the fruitful Goddess reigns,
Through all the lovely Realms of native Day,
Through all the circled Land, and circling Sea;
With fertil Seed she fill'd the pervious Earth,
And ever fix'd the mystick Ways of Birth.
Let those love now, who never lov'd before,
Let those who always lov'd, now love the more.

'Twas she the Parent, to the Latian Shore
Through various Dangers Troy's Remainder bore.
She won Lavinia for her warlike Son,
And winning her, the Latian Empire won.
She gave to Mars the Maid, whose honour'd Womb
Swell'd with the Founder of immortal Rome.
Decoy'd by Shows the Sabin Dames she led,
And taught our vig'rous Youth the Means to wed.
Hence sprung the Romans, hence the Race divine
Thro' which great Cæsar draws his Julian Line.
Let those love now, who never lov'd before,
Let those who always lov'd, now love the more.

In rural Seats the Soul of Pleasure reigns;
The Life of Beauty fills the rural Scenes;

Ev'n Love (if Fame the Truth of Love declare)
Drew first the breathings of a rural Air.
Some pleasing Meadow pregnant Beauty prest,
She laid her Infant on its flow'ry Breast,
From Nature's Sweets he sipp'd the fragrant Dew,
He smil'd, he kiss'd them, and by kissing grew.
Let those love now, who never lov'd before,
Let those who always lov'd, now love the more.

Now Bulls o'er Stalks of Broom extend their Sides,
Secure of Favours from their lowing Brides.
Now stately Rams their fleecy Consorts lead,
Who bleating follow thro' the wand'ring Shade.
And now the Goddess bids the Birds appear,
Raise all their Musick, and salute the Year:
Then deep the Swan begins, and deep the Song
Runs o'er the Water where he sails along;
While Philomela tunes a treble Strain,
And from the Poplar charms the list'ning Plain.
We fancy Love exprest at ev'ry Note,
It melts, it warbles, in her liquid Throat.
Of barb'rous Tereus she complains no more,
But sings for Pleasure as for Grief before.
And still her Graces rise, her Airs extend,
And all is Silence 'till the Syren end.

How long in coming is my lovely Spring?
And when shall I, and when the Swallow sing?
Sweet Philomela cease,—Or here I sit,
And silent lose my rapt'rous Hour of Wit:
'Tis gone, the Fit retires, the Flames decay,
My tuneful Phœbus flies averse away.
His own Amycle thus, as Stories run,
But once was silent, and that once undone.
Let those love now, who never lov'd before,
Let those who always lov'd, now love the more.

A Riddle

Upon a Bed of humble clay
In all her Garments loose
A Prostitute my Mother lay
To ev'ry Comer's use.
'Till one Gallant in heat of love
His Own Peculiar made her
And to a Region far above
And softer Beds convey'd her.
But in his Absence, to his Place
His rougher Rival came

And with a cold constrain'd Embrace
Begat me on the Dame.
I then appear'd to Publick View
A Creature wondrous bright
But shortly perishable too
Inconstant, nice and light.
On Feathers not together fast
I wildly flew about
And from my Father's country past
To find my Mother out.
Where her Gallant of her beguil'd
With me enamour'd grew
And I that was my Mother's Child
Brought forth my Mother too.

A Desire to Praise

Propitious Son of God to thee
With all my soul I bend my knee,
My wish I send my want impart,
And dedicate my mind and heart,
For as an absent parent's son
Whose second year is only run,
When no protecting friend is near,
Void of wit and void of fear,
With things that hurt him fondly plays,
Or here he falls, or there he strays;
So shou'd my soul's eternal guide
The sacred spirit be deny'd,
Thy servant soon the loss wou'd know,
And sink in sin, or run to woe.

O spirit bountifully kind,
Warm, possess, and fill my mind,
Disperse my sins with light divine
And raise the flames of love with thine,
Before thy pleasures rightly priz'd
Let wealth and honour be despis'd,
And let the Father's glory be
More dear itself than life to me.

Sing of Jesus! virgins sing
Him your everlasting King;
Sing of Jesus! chearful youth,
Him the God of love and truth:
Write and raise a song divine
Or come and hear, and borrow mine.
Son Eternal, word supreme,
Who made the universal frame,

Heav'n and all its shining show,
Earth and all it holds below;
Bow with mercy bow thine ear
While we sing thy praises here;
Son Eternal ever bless'd,
Resting on the Father's breast,
Whose tender love for all provides,
Whose power over all presides;
Bow with pity, bow thine ear
While we sing thy praises, hear.

Thou, by pity's soft extream,
Mov'd, and won, and set on flame,
Assum'd the form of man, and fell
In pains, to rescue man from hell;
How bright thine humble glories rise
And match the lustre of the skies,
From death and hell's dejected state
Arising, thou resum'd thy seat,
And golden thrones of bliss prepar'd
Above, to be thy saints reward.

How bright thy glorious honours rise,
And with new lustre grace the skies.
For thee, the sweet seraphick Choir
Raise the voice and tune the Lyre,
And praises with harmonious sounds
Through all the highest heav'n rebounds.

O make our notes with theirs agree
And bless the souls that sing of thee:
To thee, the churches here rejoice,
The solemn organs aid the voice:
To sacred roofs the sound we raise,
The sacred roofs resound thy praise:
And while our notes in one agree,
O! bless the church that sings to thee.

A Song

Thyrsis, a young and am'rous Swain,
Saw two, the Beauties of the Plain;
Who both his Heart subdue:
Gay Cælia's Eyes were dazzling fair,
Sabina's easy Shape and Air
With softer Magick drew.
He haunts the Stream, he haunts the Grove,
Lives in a fond Romance of Love,
And seems for each to dye;

'Till each a little spiteful grown,
Sabina Cælia's Shape ran down,
And she Sabina's Eye.
Their Envy made the Shepherd find
Those Eyes, which Love cou'd only blind;
So set the Lover free:
No more he haunts the Grove or Stream,
Or with a True-love Knot and Name
Engraves a wounded Tree.
Ah Cælia! (sly Sabina cry'd)
Tho' neither love, we're both deny'd;
Now, to support the Sex's Pride,
Let either fix the Dart.
Poor Girl! (says Cælia) say no more;
For shou'd the Swain but one adore,
That Spite which broke his Chains before,
Wou'd break the other's Heart.

An Allegory on Man

A thoughtful Being, long and spare,
Our Race of Mortals call him Care:
(Were Homer living, well he knew
What Name the Gods have call'd him too)
With fine Mechanick Genius wrought,
And lov'd to work, tho' no one bought.

This Being, by a Model bred
In Jove's eternal sable Head,
Contriv'd a Shape impow'rd to breathe,
And be the Worldling here beneath.

The Man rose staring, like a Stake;
Wond'ring to see himself awake!
Then look'd so wise, before he knew
The Bus'ness he was made to do;
That pleas'd to see with what a Grace
He gravely shew'd his forward Face,
Jove talk'd of breeding him on high,
An Under-something of the Sky.

But e'er he gave the mighty Nod,
Which ever binds a Poet's God:
(For which his Curls Ambrosial shake,
And Mother Earth's oblig'd to quake
He saw old Mother Earth arise,
She stood confess'd before his Eyes;
But not with what we read she wore,
A Castle for a Crown before,

Nor with long Streets and longer Roads
Dangling behind her, like Commodes:
As yet with Wreaths alone she drest,
And trail'd a Landskip-painted Vest.
Then thrice she rais'd, (as Ovid said)
And thrice she bow'd, her weighty Head.

Her Honours made, Great Jove, she cry'd,
This Thing was fashion'd from my Side;
His Hands, his Heart, his Head are mine;
Then what hast thou to call him thine?

Nay rather ask, the Monarch said,
What boots his Hand, his Heart, his Head,
Were what I gave remov'd away?
Thy Part's an idle Shape of Clay.

Halves, more than Halves! cry'd honest Care,
Your Pleas wou'd make your Titles fair,
You claim the Body, you the Soul,
But I who join'd them, claim the whole.

Thus with the Gods Debate began,
On such a trivial Cause, as Man.
And can Celestial Tempers rage?
(Quoth Virgil in a later Age.)

As thus they wrangled, Time came by;
(There's none that paint him such as I,
For what the Fabling Antients sung
Makes Saturn old, when Time was young.)
As yet his Winters had not shed
Their silver Honours on his Head;
He just had got his Pinions free
From his old Sire Eternity.
A Serpent girdled round he wore,
The Tail within the Mouth before;
By which our Almanacks are clear
That learned Ægypt meant the Year.
A Staff he carry'd, where on high
A Glass was fix'd to measure by,
As Amber Boxes made a Show
For Heads of Canes an Age ago.
His Vest, for Day, and Night, was py'd;
A bending Sickle arm'd his Side;
And Spring's new Months his Train adorn;
The other Seasons were unborn.

Known by the Gods, as near he draws,
They make him Umpire of the Cause.
O'er a low Trunk his Arm he laid,

(Where since his Hours a Dial made
Then leaning heard the nice Debate,
And thus pronounc'd the Words of Fate.

Since Body from the Parent Earth,
And Soul from Jove receiv'd a Birth,
Return they where they first began;
But since their Union makes the Man,
'Till Jove and Earth shall part these two,
To Care who join'd them, Man is due.

He said, and sprung with swift Career
To trace a Circle for the Year;
Where ever since the Seasons wheel,
And tread on one another's Heel.

'Tis well, said Jove, and for consent
Thund'ring he shook the Firmament.
Our Umpire Time shall have his Way,
With Care I let the Creature stay:
Let Bus'ness vex him, Av'rice blind,
Let Doubt and Knowledge rack his Mind,
Let Error act, Opinion speak,
And Want afflict, and Sickness break,
And Anger burn, Dejection chill,
And Joy distract, and Sorrow kill.
'Till arm'd by Care and taught to Mow,
Time draws the long destructive Blow;
And wasted Man, whose quick decay
Comes hurrying on before his Day,
Shall only find, by this Decree,
The Soul flies sooner back to Me.

The Happy Man

How bless'd the man, how fully so,
As far as man is bless'd below,
Who taking up his cross essays
To follow Jesus all his days,
With resolution to obey,
And steps enlarging in his way.
The Father of the saints above
Adopts him with a Father's love,
And makes his bosom throughly shine
With wond'rous stores of grace divine;
Sweet grace divine the pledge of joy
That will his soul above employ;
Full joy, that when his time is done
Becomes his portion as a son.

Ah me! the sweet infus'd desires
The fervid wishes, holy fires,
Which thus a melted heart refine,
Such are his and such be mine.
From hence, despising all besides
That earth reveals or ocean hides,
All that men in either prize,
On God alone he sets his eyes.
From hence his hope is on the wings,
His health renews, his safety springs,
His glory blazes up below,
And all the streams of comfort flow.

He calls his Saviour, King above,
Lord of mercy, Lord of love,
And finds a kingly care defend,
And mercy smile, and love descend,
To chear, to guide him in the ways
Of this vain world's deceitful maze:
And tho' the wicked earth display
Its terrors in their fierce array,
Or gape so wide that horrour shews
Its hell replete with endless woes;
Such succour keeps him clear of Ill
Still firm to good and dauntless still.
So fix'd, by Providence's hands
A rock amidst an ocean stands;
So bears without a trembling dread
The tempest beating round its head,
And with its side repels the wave
Whose hollow seems a coming grave;
The skies the deeps are heard to roar
The rock stands settled as before.

I, all with whom he has to do,
Admire the life which blesses you,
That feeds a foe, that aids a friend,
Without a bye designing end;
Its knowing real int'rest lies
On the bright side of yonder skies,
Where having made a title fair
It mounts and leaves the world to care.
While he that seeks for pleasing days
In earthly joys and evil ways,
Is but the fool of toil or fame,
(Tho' happy be the specious name)
And made by wealth, which makes him great,
A more conspicuous wretch of state.

On A Certain Poets Judgement Between Mr Pope & Mr Philips Don In An Italian Air

Upon a time, and in a place,
With Pan Apollo playd,
Grave Midas sat to Judge ye case,
And Pan ye Victour made.
The Rustick to his Fauns withdrew;
Whilst on ye silver wing
Sweet Phœbus for Parnassus flew
To hear his Homer sing.
Yet ere he went to Midas said,
Ile fitt you for your Jears,
So took two leaves from off his head,
And stuck them in his ears.
Tis hence he thinks the bays his own,
And hence it comes to pass
That as we think his ears are grown
We sooner find the Ass.

Dr. Parnel To Dr. Swift, On His Birth-Day, November 30th, MDCCXIII

Urg'd by the warmth of Friendship's sacred flame,
But more by all the glories of thy fame;
By all those offsprings of thy learned mind,
In judgment solid, as in wit refin'd,
Resolv'd I sing: Tho' lab'ring up the way
To reach my theme, O Swift, accept my lay.

Rapt by the force of thought, and rais'd above,
Thro' Contemplation's airy fields I rove;
Where pow'rful Fancy purifies my eye,
And lights the beauties of a brighter sky;
Fresh paints the meadows, bids green shades ascend,
Clear rivers wind, and op'ning plains extend;
Then fills its landscape thro' the vary'd parts
With Virtues, Graces, Sciences, and Arts:
Superiour Forms, of more than mortal air,
More large than mortals, more serenely fair.
Of these two Chiefs, the guardians of thy name,
Conspire to raise thee to the point of fame.
Ye Future Times, I heard the silver sound!
I saw the Graces form a circle round!
Each, where she fix'd, attentive seem'd to root,
And all, but Eloquence herself, was mute.

High o'er the rest I see the Goddess rise,
Loose to the breeze her upper garment flies:
By turns, within her eyes the Passions burn,
And softer Passions languish in their turn:

Upon her tongue Persuasion, or Command;
And decent Action dwells upon her hand.

From out her breast ('twas there the treasure lay)
She drew thy labours to the blaze of day.
Then gaz'd, and read the charms she could inspire,
And taught the list'ning audience to admire,
How strong thy flight, how large thy grasp of thought,
How just thy schemes, how regularly wrought;
How sure you wound when Ironies deride,
Which must be seen, and feign to turn aside.
'Twas thus exploring she rejoic'd to see
Her brightest features drawn so near by thee:
Then here, she cries, let future ages dwell,
And learn to copy where they can't excel.

She spake. Applause attended on the close:
Then Poesy, her sister-art, arose;
Her fairer sister, born in deeper ease,
Not made so much for bus'ness, more to please.
Upon her cheek sits Beauty, ever young;
The Soul of Music warbles on her tongue;
Bright in her eyes a pleasing Ardour glows,
And from her heart the sweetest Temper flows:
A laurel-wreath adorns her curls of hair,
And binds their order to the dancing air:
She shakes the colours of her radiant wing,
And, from the Spheres, she takes a pitch to sing.

Thrice happy Genius his, whose Works have hit
The lucky point of bus'ness and of wit.
They seem like show'rs, which April months prepare
To call their flow'ry glories up to air:
The drops descending, take the painted bow,
And dress with sunshine, while for good they flow.
To me retiring oft, he finds relief
In slowly-wasting care, and biting grief:
From me retreating oft, he gives to view
What eases care and grief in others too.
Ye fondly grave, be wise enough to know,
'Life ne'er unbent were but a life of woe.'
Some full in stretch for greatness, some for gain,
On his own rack each puts himself to pain.
I'll gently steal you from your toils away,
Where balmy winds with scents ambrosial play;
Where, on the banks as crystal rivers flow,
They teach immortal amarants to grow:
Then, from the mild indulgence of the scene,
Restore your tempers strong for toils again.

She ceas'd: Soft music trembled in the wind,

And sweet delight diffus'd thro' ev'ry mind:
The little Smiles, which still the Goddess grace,
Sportive arose, and ran from face to face.
But chief (and in that place the Virtues bless)
A gentle band their eager joys express:
Here Friendship asks, and Love of Merit longs
To hear the Goddesses renew their songs;
Here great Benevolence to Man is pleas'd;
These own their Swift, and grateful hear him prais'd.
You gentle band, you well may bear your part,
You reign Superior Graces in his heart.

O swift! if fame be life, (as well we know
That Bards and Heroes have esteem'd it so)
Thou canst not wholly die; thy works will shine
To future times, and Life in Fame be thine.

An Imitation of Some French Verses

Relentless Time! destroying Pow'r
Whom Stone and Brass obey,
Who giv'st to ev'ry flying Hour
To work some new Decay;
Unheard, unheeded, and unseen,
Thy secret Saps prevail,
And ruin Man, a nice Machine
By Nature form'd to fail.
My Change arrives; the Change I meet,
Before I thought it nigh.
My Spring, my Years of Pleasure fleet,
And all their Beauties dye.
In Age I search, and only find
A poor unfruitful Gain,
Grave Wisdom stalking slow behind,
Oppress'd with loads of Pain.
My Ignorance cou'd once beguile,
And fancy'd Joys inspire;
My Errors cherish'd Hope to smile
On newly-born Desire.
But now Experience shews, the Bliss
For which I fondly sought,
Not worth the long impatient Wish,
And Ardour of the Thought.
My Youth met Fortune fair array'd,
(In all her Pomp she shone)
And might, perhaps, have well essay'd
To make her Gifts my own:
But when I saw the Blessings show'r
On some unworthy Mind,

I left the Chace, and own'd the Pow'r
Was justly painted blind.
I pass'd the Glories which adorn
The splendid Courts of Kings,
And while the Persons mov'd my Scorn,
I rose to scorn the Things.
My Manhood felt a vig'rous Fire
By Love encreas'd the more;
But Years with coming Years conspire
To break the Chains I wore.
In Weakness safe, the Sex I see
With idle Lustre shine;
For what are all their Joys to me,
Which cannot now be mine?
But hold—I feel my Gout decrease,
My Troubles laid to rest,
And Truths which wou'd disturb my Peace
Are painful Truths at best.
Vainly the Time I have to roll
In sad Reflection flies;
Ye fondling Passions of my Soul!
Ye sweet Deceits! arise.
I wisely change the Scene within,
To Things that us'd to please;
In Pain, Philosophy is Spleen,
In Health, 'tis only Ease.

Anacreontick I

Gay Bacchus liking Estcourt's Wine,
A noble Meal bespoke;
And for the Guests that were to Dine,
Brought Comus, Love, and Joke.
The God near Cupid drew his Chair,
And Joke near Comus plac'd;
Thus Wine makes Love forget its Care,
And Mirth exalts a Feast.
The more to please the sprightly God,
Each sweet engaging Grace
Put on some Cloaths to come abroad,
And took a Waiters Place.
Then Cupid nam'd at every Glass
A Lady of the Sky;
While Bacchus swore he'd Drink the Lass,
And had it Bumper high.
Fat Comus tost his Brimmers o're,
And always got the most;
For Joke took care to fill him more,
When-e'er he mist the Toast.

They call'd, and drank at every Touch,
Then fill'd, and drank again;
And if the Gods can take too much,
'Tis said, they did so then.
Free Jests run all the Table round,
And with the Wine conspire,
(While they by sly Reflection wound,)
To set their Heads on Fire.
Gay Bacchus little Cupid stung,
By reck'ning his Deceits;
And Cupid mock'd his stammering Tongue,
With all his staggering Gaits.
Joke droll'd on Comus' greedy Ways,
And Tales without a Jest;
While Comus call'd his witty Plays,
But Waggeries at Best.
Such Talk soon set 'em all at Odds;
And, had I Homer's Pen,
I'd sing ye, how they drunk, like Gods,
And how they fought, like Men.
To part the Fray, the Graces fly,
Who make 'em soon agree;
And had the Furies selves been nigh,
They still were Three to Three.
Bacchus appeas'd, rais'd Cupid up,
And gave him back his Bow;
But kept some Darts to stir the Cup,
Where Sack and Sugar flow.
Joke taking Comus' rosie Crown,
In Triumph wore the Prize,
And thrice, in Mirth, he pusht him down,
As thrice he strove to rise.
Then Cupid sought the Myrtle Grove,
Where Venus did recline,
And Beauty close embracing Love,
They join'd to Rail at Wine.
And Comus loudly cursing Wit,
Roll'd off to some Retreat,
Where boon Companions gravely sit,
In fat unweildy State.
Bacchus and Joke, who stay behind,
For one fresh Glass prepare;
They Kiss, and are exceeding kind,
And Vow to be sincere.
But part in Time, whoever hear
This our Instructive Song;
For tho' such Friendships may be dear,
They can't continue long.

Anacreontick II

When Spring came on with fresh Delight,
To cheer the Soul, and charm the Sight,
While easy Breezes, softer Rain,
And warmer Suns salute the Plain;
'Twas then, in yonder Piny Grove,
That Nature went to meet with Love.

Green was her Robe, and green her Wreath,
Where-e'er she trod, 'twas green beneath;
Where-e'er she turn'd, the Pulses beat
With new recruits of Genial Heat;
And in her Train the Birds appear,
To match for all the coming Year.

Rais'd on a Bank, where Daizys grew,
And Vi'lets intermix'd a Blew,
She finds the Boy she went to find;
A thousand Pleasures wait behind,
Aside, a thousand Arrows lye,
But all unfeather'd wait to fly.

When they met, the Dame and Boy,
Dancing Graces, idle Joy,
Wanton Smiles, and airy Play,
Conspir'd to make the Scene be gay;
Love pair'd the Birds through all the Grove,
And Nature bid them sing to Love,
Sitting, hopping, flutt'ring, sing,
And pay their Tribute from the Wing,
To fledge the Shafts that idly lye,
And yet unfeather'd wait to fly.

'Tis thus, when Spring renews the Blood,
They meet in ev'ry trembling Wood,
And thrice they make the Plumes agree,
And ev'ry Dart they mount with three,
And ev'ry Dart can boast a Kind,
Which suits each proper turn of Mind.

From the tow'ring Eagle's Plume
The Gen'rous Hearts accept their Doom;
Shot by the Peacock's painted Eye
The vain and airy Lovers dye:
For careful Dames and frugal Men,
The Shafts are speckled by the Hen.
The Pyes and Parrots deck the Darts,
When Prattling wins the panting Hearts:
When from the Voice the Passions spring,
The warbling Finch affords a Wing:

Together, by the Sparrow stung,
Down fall the wanton and the young:
And fledg'd by Geese the Weapons fly,
When others love they know not why.

All this (as late I chanc'd to rove)
I learn'd in yonder waving Grove.
And see, says Love, (who call'd me near)
How much I deal with Nature here,
How both support a proper Part,
She gives the Feather, I the Dart:
Then cease for Souls averse to sigh,
If Nature cross ye, so do I;
My Weapon there unfeather'd flies,
And shakes and shuffles through the Skies.
But if the mutual Charms I find
By which she links you, Mind to Mind,
They wing my Shafts, I poize the Darts,
And strike from both, through both your Hearts.

A Tavern Feast

Gay Bacchus liking B---s wine
A noble meal bespoke
& for ye guests that were to dine
Brought Comus Love & Joke
The God near Cupid drew his chair
& Joke by Comus plact
Thus wine makes Love forget his care
& Mirth exalts a feast
To make it more deserve ye God
Each sweet engaging Grace
Put on some cloaths to come abroad
& took a waiters place
Then Cupid namd for ev'ry glass
A Lady of ye sky
& Bacchus swore he'd drink ye ye Lass
& had it bumper high
Fat Comus tossd his brimmers o're
& allways gott ye most
For Joke took care to fill him more
When ere he missd ye toast
They calld & drunk at evry touch
& calld & drunk again
& if ye Gods can take too much
Tis said they did so then
Free Jests ran all the table round
& with ye wine conspire
While they by sly reflections wound

To Set their heads afire
Plump Bacchus little Cupid stung
By reckning his deceits
& Cupid mockd his stammring tongue
& all his stagg'ring gates
Joke drolld on Comus Greedy ways
& tales without a Jest
& Comus calld his witty plays
But waggerys at best
such talking sett them all at odds
& had I Homers pen
Ide sing you how they drunk like Gods
& how they fought like men
To part ye fray the Graces fly
Who make them soon agree
& had ye furys selves been nigh
They still were three to three
Bacchus appeasd letts Cupid up
& gave him back his bow
But kept some darts to stirr ye Cup
Where Sack & Sugar flow
Joke taking Comus rosy crown
In triumph wore ye prize
& thrice in mirth he pushd him down
As thrice he strove to rise
Then Cupid sought ye mirtle grove
Where Venus did recline
& Beauty close embracing Love
They Joyn to rail at Wine
& Comus loudly cursing witt
Rolld off to some retreat
Where boon companions gravely sitt
In dull unwieldy state
Bacchus & Joke who stay behind
For one fresh glass prepare
& kiss & are exceeding kind
& vow to be sincere
But part in time whoever here
Are couchd within my song
For tho the friendship may be dear
It cant continue long.

Since Bearing of a Gentle Mind

Since bearing of a Gentle mind
Woud make you perfect be
Dear Celia to your self be kind
By being so to me
Hast to be happy while you can

Time flys and pleasures flow
Nor ere will have the Chance again
To be so long as now
Give me a kiss now give me more
And now another bliss
For Love has such a world in store
We need not dy on this
Twas thus Amintor Celia wood
The Fair expecting lay
He took the hint his point pursud
And blessd the lucky day.

Now Kind Now Coy wth How Much Change

Now kind now coy wth how much change
You feed my fierce desire
As if to more extravagance
Youd manage up the fire
In vain if this your meaning be
In vain you use these wayes
Tis æqually as hard for me
To love you more as less
To other nymphs bequeath yr arts
Whose eyes more faintly shine
Or practise them at least on hearts
Which love you not like mine.

www.ingramcontent.com/pod-product-compliance
Lightning Source LLC
Chambersburg PA
CBHW060146050426
42448CB00010B/2330